You're An Angel

Peter and David have written a marvellously encouraging, reassuring and above all honest account of Christian witnessing today. It's honest, and so it's full of hope. Because these guys understand that when it comes to evangelism, Christians have nothing to fear but fear itself. Be an angel, and read it!
The Revd Paul Bayes. National Mission & Evangelism Adviser,
Archbishops' Council, Church of England

You're an Angel will be an answer to prayer for any church looking for resources that will both encourage and equip members to share their faith in everyday situations. It is theologically well grounded and deeply rooted in the authors' own experience of God, and presents an honest picture of the challenges as well as the opportunities offered by a post-modern generation.
John Drane, author of The McDonaldization of the Church *and* Do Christians know how to be Spiritual? The rise of New Spirituality & the Mission of the Church *(both published by Darton Longman & Todd).*

As we struggle with the great commission in this Post Modern age, there will be a corporate sigh of relief from all who read this book. David and Peter, through their own rich and diverse experiences and naked honesty, have given us permission to express our own feelings of doubt and inadequacy as evangelists. The theme of God's love for us, and of His desire that we 'be ourselves' as we reach out, is reiterated throughout and this, alongside practical and applicable strategies for bringing our faith to the world outside our churches, should greatly encourage and equip us to 'be an angel' wherever God has placed us.
Fiona Marks
Alpha Scotland Director

YOU'RE AN ANGEL!

Being yourself and sharing your faith

by Peter Neilson and David E. P. Currie.

Covenanters

Published by
Covenanters Press
an imprint of
Zeticula
57 St Vincent Crescent
Glasgow
G3 8NQ

http://www.covenanters.co.uk
admin@covenanters.co.uk

First published November 2005
Reprinted April 2006
Reprinted April 2007

Paperback ISBN 1-905022-26-3

A catalogue record for this publication is available from the British Library. Every effort has been made to verify the accuracy of previously published quotations and to obtain permissions where appropriate. The publishers will be glad to rectify any errors or omissions in future editions.

Scripture taken from THE MESSAGE. Copyright © by Eugene H. Peterson, 1993, 1994, 1995. Used by permission of NavPress Publishing Group.

Scripture quotations are taken from the HOLY BIBLE, NEW INTERNATIONAL VERSION, copyright © 1973,1978, 1984 by International Bible Society. Used by permission of Hodder & Stoughton. All rights reserved. "NIV" is a registered trademark of International Bible Society. UK trademark number 1448790.

CONTENTS

Preface - Mapping the Way

There's an angel in the middle of ev-angel-ism.

An 'angel' is a carrier of good news.

You're an angel!

Be yourself and share your faith.

Followers *of* the Way invite others to join them **on** the Way.
That is the simple message of this book.

The point is this: God uses ordinary people as 'angels'
– messengers of good news. This book is written to make any
Christian say, 'I could do that!' We pray that God will set people
free from misconceptions and inhibitions about sharing their
faith and liberate an army of ordinary people into giving away
what they know about God. It will be Good News to somebody.
By the way, being an angel is not the same as being angelic!

David tells a great story. His life has been a journey of
discovering how to share the Good News by learning how not to
do it. With disarming honesty and earthy Glasgow humour, he
lets us laugh at him – and face our own embarrassment when
it comes to sharing our faith. He faces up to the caricatures
and encourages us to 'be ourselves' as we share our faith with
sensitivity.

That means being honest about our own struggles with faith
in the midst of life's challenges. Strange to say, people relate
better to our vulnerability than to an appearance of confidence
that we have life all sorted out. Peter and David open
themselves up to new ways of communicating the gospel.

Peter suggests that sharing our vulnerability will only happen
where there is an attitude of hospitality and acceptance. That
can be around a meal or through the welcome of our church
fellowship or the space we create for children in our churches.
We travel from Celtic monasteries to Alpha suppers in pursuit of
this gentle gift.

An accepting, welcoming atmosphere provides the setting for
the creation of community. Our society is full of lonely people
who feel dislocated and need a place to belong. The quality
of our community life as a church will offer the belonging that

must come before people consider believing in the Christ we worship and follow. Are our churches transforming communities where people find forgiveness lived out among us? Our body language is our message. Peter reminds us that there is no cheap evangelism. It is primarily living – not just talking – that is the hallmark of true community.

The ways people discover the reality of Christ are changing. We need to listen attentively rather than speak too quickly. We need the patience to share in life's journey with others rather than expect everyone to have some crisis moment of discovery. People want to explore spirituality rather than argue over beliefs. David spells out some of these changes in a very clear way and Peter shares some practical examples of where he has seen these principles at work.

Peter reminds us that everyone loves a good story and every Christian has a story to tell. When we are in touch with the story of what God means to us in our own lives, then, like witnesses in court, we can tell our story publicly to others. David encourages us to tell our story among the networks of people who make up our daily lives.

For Peter, one of the key points of connection today is the issue of identity. There is a great deal of confusion over the search for identity. This is resolved in discovering that we are loved by God and have a new identity as children of God through being brothers and sisters of Jesus Christ. Throughout life there are moments when our fragile identities crack open, allowing God to give us a new beginning. We need to be alert to these moments in ourselves and in others.

The quest for spirituality today suggests a remarkable openness in our society. Are we are willing to walk alongside people, win their trust and share what we have as fellow travellers and fellow seekers? If we dare to be truly ourselves, we can dare to believe that God will be truly himself, and that he will turn up in ways that will surprise us. When people discover the reality of

God and recognise the Risen Christ, it is sheer mystery. There is no formula. David introduces us to the Essence course and the Labyrinth as ways of discovery for the seeker.

How does all this play out in our workaday lives? People are looking for a spirituality that will hold together our fragmented existence. Sharing faith involves showing that Christ makes a difference to our everyday relationships, not least in the arena of work where most people spend most of their time. We want to help people discover and live out an integrated faith and find God at work. Peter shares insights from his work in business ministry.

David opens our eyes to the spiritual themes in contemporary literature, music and film. These are the places where religious themes are aired publicly. If we keep in touch with our culture, there will be many opportunities for fruitful conversations about the big issues of life. The creativity of our culture inspires us towards greater creativity in our worship and communication as Christian people who worship a God of infinite creativity.

Throughout this study, we learn from each other through exercises and discussion starters. We learn the way of Jesus – sitting with him at a business lunch with Matthew, the accountant, or asking if life's foundations have been so shaken that we need to rebuild on a new foundation. We sit with the woman at the well. We share a private moment with Zacchaeus. We end sharing a short journey with Jesus on the road to Emmaus. He listens to the questions. He tells God's big story. He sits at a table. He surprises us with his presence. Jesus on the Emmaus Road is our role model for sharing faith today.

1. The Way

'I persecuted followers of this Way.'

The Apostle Paul [1].

---

[1] Acts 22:4

Jesus – today

'Followers of this Way' was Paul's description of the first Christians. Our minds jump immediately to Jesus' claim that he was 'the Way' to the Father. No wonder Paul wanted to silence these sectarian upstarts.

Today it is not the iron fist of persecution that silences Christians, but the velvet glove of political correctness. In our wonderfully interconnected world of many faiths and worldviews, it feels distinctly uncomfortable to make special claims for Jesus of Nazareth as 'the Way'. Much better, surely, to speak of Jesus as 'a way' among many. So the argument goes.

Embarrassment about our history freezes us over at the mouth. Christianity and colonial conquest have meshed together into a bind of guilt. How did we ever confuse the crucified Jesus with the way of power? How did the One who attacked the corrupting influence of power in his own religious establishment become co-opted as the patron of institutionalised religion?

Move among the power-sensitive post-modern generation and they will smell religious manipulation at a hundred metres. They may munch their burgers dressed in their GAP sweaters while they tell you so, but any cocktail of religion and power is marked "poison"!

We recognise that any book on sharing faith today seems to be "holed below the water line" before it starts. So - can we retrace our steps, picking our way through the pick-and-mix world of our push-button culture, clamber over the mass of thumbscrews, swords and cross-bearing flags, and run the gauntlet of the historical and cultural snipers, till we are back where Jesus started – among ordinary people discovering God in a new way because this man was different?.

Jesus life-bringer

The first followers of the Way were no heroes. They had their doubts and fears and failures just like us. But travelling with this man opened doors in the imagination that had never been opened before. He helped them see a new world coming in on the wind of the Spirit. He sidestepped the movers and shakers to spend time with the moved out and the shaken up. He put a smile on the faces of children and gave dignity to abused women. His touch brought dead limbs to life and his words sparked the life of God in people who thought God had given up on them.

There were Twelve who knew the inside story. They enjoyed the meals and the laughter. They also saw the nights of prayer and the tears of frustration. They wanted to protect him from himself, but he kept giving and giving and giving – until the day when he gave all on the Cross. No power, but what authority! No blame! Only forgiveness! The only person he would not save was himself!

Three dark days. One world-changing morning. Mary told them first. Then Peter and John. Then the couple from Emmaus. Then Thomas had his special moment.

This man was back from the dead. Nobody else had done that. Nobody else has done it since. Alive. Beyond the grip of death. Speaking from the 'coming world' of God's kingdom about forgiveness and eternal life. Inviting people who were walking into the sunset of life to turn and face the rising dawn of Resurrection life.

Jesus – Spirit-giver

Life flowed from Jesus to the Twelve through the gift of the Holy Spirit. Now it was their turn to travel the Way that Jesus had pioneered, all the way through the Cross-shaped moments of life into that same Resurrection life with God.

They were not to travel the Way alone. On the journey they were to invite others to be followers of the Way. In little clusters they moved around the Roman world. When one stumbled, another would lift him up. When the doubts were too dark for one, another would hold out the light of faith.

As they travelled, seeds of the good news fell to the ground, or blew in the wind, and new followers of the Way were mysteriously born in places far beyond their reach and beyond their ken. That blustery wind of the Spirit broke through again and again.

It was not a military campaign. It was a journey – sometimes intentional, but often driven by the changing fortunes of the time, moving from place to place.

It was not a solo venture. It was the activity of a community of people who welcomed others and showed the kindness of God in a callous world.

It was not a professional presentation. It was a company of ordinary people who told the story of the Jesus whose Way they were following. They told their story in market and in home because it belonged there. Jesus belongs there.

It was not a programme. It was a messy, untidy, life-shaped movement of people who, with infinite creativity, engaged in conversation, wrote letters and books, drew carvings in catacombs, devised ways of celebrating and remembering, and watched God bring life to others through their words and actions.

There is no sophisticated theology of evangelism in this little book. We aim to be followers of the Way of Jesus. From time to time you will be invited to pause and learn from Jesus or the followers of Jesus by reading a section of a Gospel or the story of Acts. We pray that by rubbing shoulders with them, you might recover or discover the energy and desire to pass on the story to others.

All we ask is that you travel this Way with Jesus. Stay close to Him and His Way and others will come close to know more.

Do not be afraid. Even if the politically correct persecutors do pounce, remember what happened to Paul! Remember that across the world, Christians are suffering for their faith – and we do believe in resurrection – don't we?.

2. The Way of Ordinary People

'An army of ordinary people.'

Dave Bilborough[2]

---

[2] First line of a song by Dave Bilborough, Thank You Music, 1983.

DAVID:

Wow! A book on 'sharing your faith'?
And Peter Neilson and I should have a
crack at it? At first I was just so excited
about the possibilities:

• This is just what the church in Scotland
needs at this time

• Another well-respected colleague (Rev
Stewart Matthew) had written a couple of
down-to-earth books before he died all too
suddenly – *Leading God's People* and *Caring
for God's People*. These had certainly been
appreciated by my own elders and members
when I was a minister in East Kilbride West
Kirk and a friend had shared that Stewart's
intention was to have written a third in the
series – *Evangelising God's People*.

It was only after a bit of a struggle (do we really need another
book on evangelism?) and a bit of prayer that I eventually
arrived at an altogether more settled and relaxed place about
the whole project. Reaching out to others had been at the
centre of my own ministry for seventeen years in East Kilbride
West Kirk where our congregation experienced significant
growth. Even before that, my early Christian years had been
influenced by going on seaside mission with my home church
(Moncreiff Parish Church in East Kilbride) – helping with the
beach mission for kids, doing a talk at the Youth Café, sharing
some banter about my own journey to faith as part of the
evening sing-along at the harbour. Aye, North Berwick and
Stranraer have never been the same since!

Then in August 2000, I took up the post of Senior Adviser in Mission and Evangelism for the Church of Scotland and my conviction - that mission has to be at the heart of church - has never been stronger. Mission has to be at the heart of church because mission is in the heart of God.

My work now takes me all over Scotland, and indeed sometimes to other parts of the world. But still a Glasgow boy at heart, I was starting to get very excited about the possibility of a Scottish contribution to the many helpful resources on sharing our faith with others – this would be an attempt to address the real missionary opportunity that faces us in Scotland today, and in order to be useful to as many people as possible, it would have to be 'down to earth'.

For all sorts of reasons we'll look at later, 'evangelism' can get really bad press and for many folk in our churches, it has negative connotations. (One colleague visiting a church was warned, 'Please don't mention the "e-word" here!')

So, before looking at some of the facts and before our examination of what mission and evangelism should be (and what they shouldn't!) I want to start by drawing your attention to the five letters which make up the small word right in the middle of the longer word, 'evangelism'. I want to start this whole enterprise by reminding you that —

there's an ANGEL in the middle
of ev-angel-ism

In the Bible an angel is usually the bearer of good news – think of the Christmas story:

> An angel of the Lord appeared to them, and the glory of the Lord shone over them. They were terribly afraid, but the angel said to them, 'Don't be afraid! I am here with good news for you, which will bring great joy to all the people. This day in David's town your Saviour was born – Christ the Lord! And this is what will prove it to you: you will find a baby wrapped in strips of cloth and lying in a manger.'
> Luke 2:9-12

And is it always "special beings" that God uses to spread His 'good news'? No. The disciples were pretty ordinary folk, after all. Often, God uses ordinary people like you and me.

You're an angel

• when you visit your neighbour in hospital

• when you help a blind person across the road

• when you make the coffee for the boys at work

• when you cut "their" side of the hedge

• when you phone to see how I'm doing

• when you stop to help someone with a puncture

• when you offer to help with "the hen nite"

• when you give a word of comfort

• when you make the dinner for the family (again!)

• when you do all sorts of volunteer work – **you're an angel**

And the list could go on and on – it's a list that includes you and me. 'But I was never trying to get anyone into church! Fine, that's OK! 'But I always thought evangelism, sharing the good news, mission, was only something done by certain gifted people.' Well, you thought wrong!

So evangelism is in fact a fantastic word which includes all the talking and doing by certain special or gifted people and by ordinary punters, consciously and unconsciously – anyone who's spreading God's love and kindness, usually putting others before themselves. 'You're an angel.'

You're an angel!

In what ordinary ways might you have been used
to share God's good news in the form
of care and kindness?

Well, how's that for starters, Peter? You must have come across a lot of angels in your own work?

PETER:

Yes, David. When I was a minister in Glasgow, I used to have a weekly Enquirers' Class for people who wanted to explore the Christian Faith. At some point along the way, I would ask what had prompted people to come. One young woman replied: 'I'm here because I live next door to an angel!'

Her neighbour was one of those wee "Glesca buddies" who had made her welcome when she moved into the street as a young bride. When the children were born she was always ready to baby-sit and let the harassed young mum out for a few precious hours on her own. If she was going to the shops, she rang the bell to see if she could get anything for her hard-pressed neighbour.

Our 'angel' was a regular worshipper and real worker in the church, along with her husband, who was known for his great organising abilities. Between them, they were a marvellous example of practical Christianity.

Several years down the line, this young woman was starting on a serious journey to faith in Christ. Her 'angel' next door would have been embarrassed at the description. She would have laughed, but she would have been thrilled to think that her little acts of kindness had become stepping stones for her young friend to find Christ.

At the opening of a Scottish School of Evangelism in 1993, the then Moderator of the General Assembly, Hugh Wyllie, described evangelism in three short phrases: 'Be the Story. Do the Story. Tell the Story.'

It takes all three modes of communication to get the message across. Just think of Jesus – 'the Word became a human being and moved into the neighbourhood' – being God's word, acting out God's word and speaking God's word. He is the good news present in word and action.

One rural minister was once describing his church and how people were coming to faith in a steady stream. He spoke of the place that young people had in the worship. His guild prayed for every child who had been baptised until they went to school. There were regular opportunities for prayer and Bible Study. He mentioned in the passing a 90-year-old lady who was housebound and how people took turns to visit and do her shopping. There was a healing group who regularly prayed for the sick in the village. One church elder had gone to learn British Sign Language because one of the members in her care had gone stone deaf.

When asked about any intentional approaches to evangelism, he looked puzzled. 'I don't think we have any!' The whole body language of that village church was expressing the good news of Jesus Christ. People caught the good infection of the gospel from the Christians going about their everyday life.

We make the business of sharing faith too complicated. One congregation, for example, was preparing to embark on a special mission to their community. They turned up faithfully for five weeks to be trained for the job. At the end of that time, the minister's wife reckoned they were more anxious than they had been at the outset. They were more aware of what they might do wrong!

Gavin Reid catches the right spirit when he says:

> When all is said and done, evangelism happens when people simply share with others what it is about God which excites them or which they find helpful.[3]

A few years ago, my wife and I were on holiday on the Isle of Skye. We were staying in bed and breakfast accommodation where guests all ate at the one large, round table. Conversation turned to our various occupations. I owned up reluctantly to being a minister.

A young Swiss chemist sitting across from me immediately flared into an aggressive challenge that no intelligent person could believe in God these days. Well, I am not very good at theology over my early morning bacon and eggs. As I was moving my sluggish brain into gear, I heard a voice from beside me: 'All I know is that if God was not real, I could not make it through the day.' The voice was my wife. End of argument.

At the end of the day we returned to the B & B for dinner. The Swiss atheist was gone. The only people at the table were two American lawyers from Washington.

As we moved to coffee, the man commented that he had been impressed by what had been said at breakfast. When we asked what he meant, he said: 'Nothing you said. It was what your wife said. You are paid to talk about God. I have never heard a minister's spouse speak so honestly about her faith.'.

[3] Reid, Gavin, *Redescribing Evangelism*, British Council of Churches, 1989, p 2

It turned out that these two highly intelligent lawyers had been longstanding agnostics, but for the next two hours we shared in a fascinating conversation about God and life today – and how God was helping my wife to cope with a period of serious depression. Her quip was no cheap shot to win a point. It was a spontaneous word from the heart about how helpful God had been in her time of darkness.

Learning from Jesus

Read the account of the first flurry of gossip about Jesus.
John 1:40-46
With whom do you identify in this story?
Is it really as easy as it sounds?

Yes, David, she is an angel! But, if I'm honest, I don't feel much of an angel myself.

DAVID:

Just be yourself! When I was a younger Christian I thought God wanted me to be just like … well… whoever my most recent 'hero' was. Imagine my relief then, when it started to dawn on me – God doesn't want you to be Billy Graham! That's Billy Graham's job. God wants you to be – YOU!

It would be a dull life if we were all the same. It's variety that makes the world interesting. That's what makes church challenging. That's what makes you unique. So when it comes to sharing your faith or witnessing for Christ:

Relax and Just Be Yourself!

Actually, this is the most challenging task that faces you and me – not getting to know the people you're sharing your faith with, not even getting to know God, but getting to know ME!

How do I know? Because it's our human condition – not facing our faults, but covering them up, doing anything I can sometimes to avoid facing up to the real me. Genesis 3 is basically the story of a 'cover-up job'!

> As soon as they had eaten it, they
> were given understanding and realised
> that they were naked; so they sewed
> fig leaves together and covered
> themselves. Genesis 3:7

And that's how some of us spend most of our lives – as a

'cover-up' job. Some of you may have seen that film with Jim Carey – *The Mask.* Without the mask, the main character was an ordinary guy with not too much confidence, just trying to get on with life. But once he put the mask on, he assumed a totally different personality – 'It's time to paaartyyy!' That's you and me. Just a couple of vodka and cokes then I'll get up and dance.

Healthy Boundaries

Of course, we don't want to open up all of ourselves to any 'Tom, Dick and Harry'. Some people have a very poor self-image, very weak boundaries, and in opening up too readily to anyone, they are in real danger of inviting in all sorts of abuse.

But it's the other side of the equation I want to think about for a moment – because the mask is so firmly in place with most of us that we've lost all sense of who we really are. Some stuff (the kind of stuff I referred to earlier) is buried so deep that 'I don't even know myself properly any more'. Who are you, really?

So just for a moment –

> forget you're an engineer or student or whatever
>
> forget you're a parent
>
> forget you're a sportsperson
>
> forget you're healthy
>
> forget you're ill
>
> forget you're a church-goer
>
> forget you're a Christian
>
> forget God!(for a very short moment!)

Put all the masks to one side just for a moment or two.

Who are YOU?

Not so angelic!

Another 'moment of awakening' for me came when I did the Counselling Skills course at the Tom Allan Centre in Glasgow.

Well, well – it was certainly a help to have some of your strengths confirmed; but what a shocker to have to put down on paper or to have to share with your support group a little bit about your impatience, your untidiness or tidiness, how annoying others might find your little ways, your sexuality and your lust, your bigotry, your murderous intentions … It all came out! And I was beginning to think that people outside prison were more dangerous than people inside!

Then the really mind-blowing thing - God accepts me just like this. *'Just as I am'* is the way the hymn puts it. With all my masks and hang-ups, God accepts me, forgives me and gives me new life and new power. Not to become perfect all at once! But to allow his Holy Spirit to start knocking some of the rough edges off, to start turning me into the David Currie he wants me to be. This is God's grace – it was 'while we were still sinners Christ died for us.'(Romans 5:8)

The Journey

Let me try to break down a typical spiritual journey (so far as many Christians are concerned) to illustrate the difference between a false idealised view of our lives and the more likely real outcome for the person whose life is dedicated to God.

Idealised View

What I was like before meeting Jesus - human, sinner, bad
Meaningful encounter with God   - the divine bit
What I'm like now   - 'new being',
                                       goody-goody

Real View

What I was like before meeting Jesus - human, mix of
                                       good and bad

Meaningful encounter with God   - I can't, God can,
                                       I'm going to let Him

What I'm like now   - still human, but
                                     with a sharpened
                                       sense of my own
                                       sinfulness and of
                                       God's grace

Learning from Jesus

Peter could get it so right and then so wrong!
Matthew 16: 13-23

Why do you think Peter 'switched channels'?
What reassurance do you find in this story?.

Relax

I know I can be 'a pain in the backside' to some people. I'm honestly beginning to face up to the different aspects of my character - some are OK and lead to appropriate behaviour; some are not so good and all too often lead to inappropriate (even embarrassing!) behaviour. My kids and my wife, however, accept me as I am - though they're not afraid to challenge me at times – and I know I can be myself with them.

There are times when I need to relax in God's presence with all of this. In times of quiet meditation and prayer I offer up to God all that I am, ask him to help me let go of all that is destructive, and ask him to develop, grow and enhance all that could be more loving, authentic and just; so that I might become more like Jesus, more the David Currie I'm supposed to be.

And it doesn't happen overnight – it's a life's journey. If it's going to be that long for me, it will be the same for anyone else. Don't be impatient. Others will take their own time.

Our part is simply to be honest about who we are and what God means to us. Just be yourself in Christ and Christ will be himself in you.

And you will become an 'angel'!

Who am I?

1. Take a sheet of paper and jot down your strengths.
    Be as honest and wide-ranging as you can be.

2. Now jot down your weaknesses.

3. If you're part of a group it really helps to share some
    of these things. Some is better shared with a close
    friend in confidence.

3. The Way of Sensitivity

'Lastly, men came, led by Christ

To build a home for restless souls

A beacon to send forth his light.'

Northumbrian Office [4]

---

[4] *Celtic Daily Prayer - A Northumbrian Office*, Marshall Pickering, 1994 p 43

PETER:

Ah, but David, other people do not share our enthusiasm for sharing this good news! Listen to this…

In a county town in north-east Scotland, a church group had gathered to prepare for visiting people in their community. As the morning of preparation passed, the anxiety levels rose tangibly, so the group leader asked everyone to form buzz groups to discuss what they feared most about this venture. The response was unanimous.

They did not want to be like the Jehovah's Witnesses. Their experience of these door-to-door visitors was of being pressurised in a way that made them feel uncomfortable. Our visitors did not want to create a similar impression. People saw this simple evangelistic task as a form of religious salesmanship. So we got to work on examining what it was that we were actually attempting to do; and once we had replaced the images of pressure and insistence with attitudes of respect and invitation, the day went with a swing!

On another occasion, in a seminar on evangelism, one woman showed a real sense of discomfort. She had come with a friend but didn't want to be involved in this 'evangelism' stuff. We jokingly insisted that the workshop would be in three stages:

> Stage 1 – Learn to build your own soapbox rather than use someone else's.
>
> Stage 2 – Learn how to hold on to the other person's lapels so that they cannot run away.
>
> Stage 3 – Learn how to force a large-sized Bible down a medium-sized throat!

After a moment of panic, she laughed and entered into the rest of the day with enthusiasm. There are so many myths around about evangelism as the hard sell. We hope that our approach to sharing the good news of God's love will avoid these negative reactions and allow you to just be yourself! And dare to believe that God will turn up in the conversation.

Time to Think

Think of an experience of evangelism which had a high cringe factor for you.

What was it that you did not like?

Come on, David. Back over to you to persuade us that we are all in the good news business!

DAVID:

Well, for me it all starts with the belief that mission is at the very heart of God, that God is a sending God and that evangelism should essentially be a thoughtful, generous, compassionate sharing of the good news.

But evangelism has had such negative press that I want just to take a few moments to say WHAT IT'S NOT.

a. Billboard man

I remember them in Glasgow way back, and they're still around today. But the one who sticks in my mind looked like a lovely, gentle old man with grey hair and a winning smile.

> Having moved to East Kilbride, my mum really missed her own mother in Glasgow, so my wee brother and I were taken in on the No. 180 bus every Saturday. We'd be making our way from Clyde Street to St. Enoch's subway station to get the tube to Cessnock station next to my Gran's house in Brand Street, so this man must have worked the Argyll Street area.
>
> Anyway, all I remember is this nice wee man walking towards us with these boards on his front and back. The message on the front was hard enough – 'Repent and be baptised …'. But did he know how to knock you for six when he was walking away from you! The sobering message continued on his back – '… for the unbeliever will be condemned for all eternity to the fiery pits of hell!'
>
> Well, I was only about eleven or twelve, and it certainly didn't turn me onto Jesus (but hey, there are some who can trace their starting point to precisely this style of evangelism.)

b. Winning knock-down arguments

Then in my late teens I invited Christ into my own life and it was the most significant thing that ever happened to me. But I was a new disciple and I really wanted other people to know about this loving God who could bring meaning and purpose to your life; as I say, I was a new disciple and I was about to make plenty mistakes.

Nothing was more important to me than that people should be told about Jesus. At that time one of my 'heroes' was an American evangelist who took a three-metre cross to different events all over the world - Arthur Blessit had just been to a variety of venues in the U.K. and I had the stickers all over my jacket, guitar and rucksack: 'Smile – God loves you' (my friend, now brother-in-law, nearly disowned me on holiday on Islay).

And now that I had God and the world all sorted out in my own head (as you do when you're in your late teens and early twenties), all I needed to do was win the argument, win the debate, and winning the people must surely follow!

Here are a couple of not-so-happy memories. I'm already cringing at the thought of sharing these stories with you but I just know you'll be sympathetic.

> My future brother-in-law and I found ourselves in the living room with his dad (my future father-in-law) and we started to tell him how important our new life in Jesus was to us. (How on earth did we work that into the relaxed after-dinner banter?) It was a brilliant discussion; I'm sure we won "the argument from design" and a few others about morals and stuff, but we somehow sensed we were 'getting nowhere'. In frustration we blurted out, 'Well the choice is either being with God in heaven or going somewhere else.' (Did we say that? I can't believe we said that.) Anyway the response ended the discussion: 'If that's the kind of God you believe in, then you can keep him!'.

But I'm thick skinned – or maybe just 'thick'! Forget friends and family, go for work-mates! I was working in Rolls Royce at the time and the guys there were brilliant – down-to-earth, a good laugh, good engineers and technicians, but I wasn't too sure if they had given their lives to God.

> Five of us were crammed into the car one Saturday morning on the way back from five-a-side football – fantastic, they can't get away, a 'captive audience'. And they started it by asking why I wasn't on the rota for the 'soft porn' material (top-shelf magazines and videos), and what was all this about reading the Bible at lunchtime? I can't remember the details of how some of the discussion went, but I remember getting it round to talking about how Jesus, God's only Son, willingly and uniquely gave his life and sacrificed himself on the cross for us so that we could get back to God. (There, that should do it.)

> Then came the exasperated reply of one of the guys who had heard just about enough of the 'question – answer, then you'll believe in God' approach: 'F---in' Japanese kamikaze pilots sacrificed their lives during the war for what they believed was a greater cause. That's not unique ya daft bandit!' (or words to that effect).

You'll have your own 'horror' stories no doubt and they are an important part of the mix, because you have to learn from your mistakes.

Go Gently

I think Steve Sjogren is absolutely right when he says that this misplaced enthusiasm to 'close the deal' probably comes from a mistaken view of evangelism. He argues that the great apostle Paul himself, deeply disappointed with the lack of response to his preaching ('a few became followers … and believed' – Acts 17:34), had to change his entire view of evangelism as a result of his experiences. This is God's work done in God's power, in God's way and in God's time:

> Paul no longer put his trust in finely crafted words. He said, 'My speech and my preaching were not with persuasive words of human wisdom, but in demonstration of the Spirit and of power' (1 Cor. 2: 4). …Paul now clearly perceived an important truth: only the Holy Spirit can bring a person to faith.

> He goes on to make it clear that evangelism is a process: 'I have planted, Apollos watered, but God gave the increase. So then neither he who plants is anything, nor he who waters, but God who gives the increase '(1 Cor. 3:6-7). Human beings can play an important role in bringing the good news to others, but it is God alone who is the real evangelist.

> When we talk about evangelism, we aren't generally talking about the planting-watering-harvesting cycle that Paul describes. We usually mean the results – the harvest alone. In fact we have become so completely preoccupied with this last phase of the evangelism process that it has tainted our approach to bringing people to Christ.[5]

So, to get back to your initial point, Peter, I do believe we're in the 'good news' business, but that doesn't mean we have to turn it into 'hard-sell' news. That doesn't only put me off sharing it. That puts them off hearing it!.

[5] Steve Sjogren, *Conspiracy of Kindness*, Vine Books, 1993, p. 122

Learning from Jesus

Seed-sowing was Jesus' picture for communication.
Mark 4:1-20
What frustrations do you find when sharing the gospel?
What are your expectations when you share the gospel?

It's a 'turn-off'

You see, people aren't daft, and they can be really suspicious of folk shoving things down their throats. Nick Spencer (a researcher with the London Institute for Contemporary Christianity) has recently produced some very helpful research which shows ironically that **evangelism itself can be a barrier to belief!**

> Tactless evangelism is second only to intolerance as a modern sin. Even on the back of selfless community service and careful relationship building it is a dangerous business, with the receiver often having antennae highly sensitive to expectations. In our religiously hostile culture, even the most undemanding and selfless servant evangelism may provoke suspicion.

> This was most clearly evident in the examples given by some respondents who spoke of the use of Christian 'services' in a tone which sometimes bordered on contempt. No matter how open, free, kindly or genuine the offering might be, the merest

41

hint that the 'service providers' might want to share
their faith was enough to bring down the full force
of some respondents' loathing. 'They want you to
come and do their sessions … they are saying, 'Do
you have any questions about God?' 'No, I've just
come here to play with my child.' (Female, 25 – 44,
London)

This natural antipathy towards being 'evangelised'
in any way, even on the back of relationships built
through community services, meant that more
naked evangelism was completely out of the
question. Ramming it 'down your throat' was among
the worst of sins.[6]

So we start with this note of caution. Go easy - take your time.
It's a point well made by Rebecca Manley Pippert in what I think
is one of the most moving treatises on evangelism to come out
of the latter part of the twentieth century.

Of course I wanted my friends to know about
God. But every time I got up courage to be vocal
about Jesus, an image leaped into my mind of an
aggressive Christian buttonholing an unwitting
victim. As a non-believer I had thought many
Christians were weird, spreading leaflets on street
corners and nabbing strangers. I was terrified that if
I said anything at all about Christ, my friends would
consider me just as strange. And I would agree
with them. There was part of me that secretly felt
evangelism was something you shouldn't do to your
dog, let alone a friend.[7]

[6] Nick Spencer, *Beyond Belief? Barriers and Bridges to Faith Today*, 2003, The London Institute
for Contemporary Christianity, pp.24 & 25
[7] Rebecca Manley Pippert, *Out of the Saltshaker*, Inter-Varsity Press, 1980,pp. 15 & 16

Over to You!

*Have you ever been in the position where you
were expected to share your faith?
How did it go?*

**Peter, can you help us to be a bit
more positive again?**

PETER:

Awakening Faith in Jesus Christ

One reason why people are so resistant
to the wrong approach in evangelism is
because it comes over to them as a kind
of power game. People in our culture
are highly sensitive to the misuse of
power. They know when they are being
patronised. They even hear claims about
'truth' as a lever of power.

If our message is about the grace of God, then it must be
shared in that same spirit of grace by coming alongside people.
Sometimes that means finding come common ground or
common concern before we share anything at all.

Raymond Fung was an industrial evangelist in Hong Kong
before taking up the role of Secretary of Evangelism with the
World Council of Churches. After travelling the world and facing
up to the deep secularisation of the West, he came to a helpful
description of evangelism:

> To evangelise is to set the context for the awakening
> or reawakening of faith in Jesus Christ.

Fung suggests that we begin on a broad canvas with the good news of hope for people who feel the world is collapsing about their ears. He takes God's vision of society described in Isaiah 65 as the New Jerusalem [8] – a society where children do not die young, where the old grow old with dignity, where every person has a home and work that is satisfying and violence has become a thing of the past.

He suggests that we join forces with any person, group or agency which is working to that agenda. We believe in a God who wants a better world and we are prepared to commit ourselves to that goal. Partnership means coming alongside others to work shoulder to shoulder for the same objectives.

We share the same goals, but we do not share the same motivation. From time to time we need to be re-energised for the work. For the Christian that means worship. Worship refocuses our vision on God who has become known to us in Jesus Christ. As we withdraw to worship, our partners will raise questions about this God who inspires us.

[8] Fung, Raymond, The Isaiah Agenda, WCC Publications, 1992

Worship may be as formal as a church service or as informal as an agape meal with friends at home. The touchstone of true worship is whether we are transformed and are moved to transform God's world. According to the same prophet Isaiah, false worship is detached from these realities.[9]

Out of these questions may come an invitation to discipleship as we invite people to consider the claims of Jesus Christ today. This journey of discipleship may involve a long-term mentoring, or sharing in a group of fellow travellers or becoming part of a local church.

This approach has been spelt out in more detail by Ann Morisy in her book on community ministry called *Beyond the Good Samaritan*. She sees community ministry as a strategy for mission that:

- enables people to act like Christians

- feeds people's imagination so that the significance of the gospel can be sensed

- can be a force of positive change in society [10]

A recent writer compares this approach to a football game. The evangelist wants to score goals by going in a straight line to the goal. The community minister operates on the wing, but knows when to pass the ball to the evangelist who is now in the penalty box, waiting to head the ball home. The action of community ministry has opened up a space in the secular imagination for the possibility of a God who is good. When that door in the imagination is opened, people are then able to receive the story of the One who is the true image of God.[11]

---

[9] See Isaiah 58

[10] Morisy, Ann, *Beyond the Good Samaritan: Community Ministry and Mission*, Mowbray, 1997, p 5

[11] Booker, Mike and Ireland, Mark, *Evangelism - which way now?*, Church House Publishing, 2003 p 95

At this point Raymond Fung would move us from the prophet Isaiah to the Gospel of Luke and to a set of stories that still echo around the secular memory: the story of the lost sheep, the lost coin and the lost son.[12]

Here is the double dynamic of God's engagement with people: seeking to find those who are lost and waiting to welcome those who come home to the Father's love – what he describes as 'active waiting and buoyant expectancy'.[13]

Even if some churches find it hard to engage in the 'seeking to find' aspect, the challenge remains to our level of prayerful and practical expectancy. Does the returning seeker find the warm embrace of the welcoming Father or the cold shoulder of the elder brother?

Learning from Jesus

Look at the audience when Jesus told these stories.
Luke 15:1-2

What would be the reaction of the different groups?

Whom do you find most/least responsive to the good news?

---

[12] Luke Chapter 15
[13] Fung, Raymond, *Evangelising a Secular Society - Europe*, essay in Ed. Samuel, Vinay, and Hauser, Albrecht, *Proclaiming Christ in Christ's Way, Studies in Integral Evangelism* Regnum Books, 1989

Apple Pie Evangelism!

Imagine an apple pie cut into three equal slices. The first slice is called people. The second slice is called story. The third slice is called prayer. Around the crust is the word, time.

That image represents for me what it means to 'set the context for the awakening or reawakening of faith in Jesus Christ.'

> • People discover God among people who are discovering God. As we will see later, over 80% of people come to faith through a personal relationship[14], usually the influence of a friend or a member of the family, or through encountering a group of Christians which intrigues them.

> • Somewhere along the line they come in touch with the story of God's love for the world as seen in Jesus Christ. That may be a personal testimony or a film or a book or some contact with the Bible. They may hear a talk or share in a discussion, but somewhere along the line God's story connects with their story, often through relating personally to our story. Hence our encouragement to 'tell it like it is' for you, and let God do the rest.

> • Prayer is somewhere in the mix. That may be the prayers of concerned friends or family who are praying with that 'buoyant expectancy' for God to make himself known in a way the seeker will recognise. It also stands for that searching spirituality which is so wide-spread today and may be no more than an unspoken ache in a person's heart [15].

14 Finney, John, *Finding Faith Today -How does it happen?,* Bible Society, 1992
15 *Ibid* p 35 where Finney claims that 60% pray before becoming Christians..•

Time stands for two significant views of time. There is time as it appears on a clock or calendar. (The Greeks called this *'chronos'*.) Research suggests that the average time for a person to move from a position of 'non-faith' to a place of commitment is likely to be four years.[16] That means that we all need to be patient and travel the journey with the person, waiting God's time.

But there is the other sense of time that is implied in our picture – God's time of opportunity. (The Greeks called this *'kairos'*.) It is important that we are sensitive to the shifts in people's views of God, and the moments along the way when they are ready to respond to the invitation and call of Jesus Christ. It is important that none of us misses that 'kairos'. Again research suggests that one third of us will be able to date that moment, while two thirds will be more aware of a slow process of discovery [17] – less like Paul's conversion on the Damascus Road, and more like the awakening of the couple on the Emmaus Road.

Be patient. Treat people gently. God does.

Time to Think

Have you seen people 'awaken' to faith in Jesus Christ? If so, describe one or two of these occasions. What factors stand out for you as being significant?

16 *Ibid* p 25
17 *Ibid* p 24

4. The Way of Vulnerability

'God did not become a man.
God became a baby.'
John Drane.

DAVID:

> Then Jesus began to teach his disciples:
> 'The Son of Man must suffer much and be
> rejected by the elders, the chief priests,
> and the teachers of the Law. He will be put
> to death, but three days later he will rise to
> life.' He made this very clear to them.
>
> Mark 8:31 & 32a

Can you believe it? It's always amazed me, the way that Mark leads to the climax of his Gospel at chapter 8, verse 29, when, after all the miracles and the excitement and the good stuff, Peter at last sees the truth - 'You are the Messiah.' And just when the disciples think they've got it sussed, life is going to be all miracles and excitement and 'living in the presence' - then, right there, at that high-point - Jesus deals them a body blow: 'the Son of Man must *suffer* much… *He will be put to death* …'.

Evangelism starts to become more real when it's 'vulnerable evangelism'. In a booklet by the same name Canon John Holmes shares a telling story about the way we're often tempted to do evangelism.

> I had been at a Church meeting specifically to speak
> about evangelism. As part of the presentation I
> had shown various statements about mission and
> evangelism which I felt could be helpful. One was
> the remark of St. Francis of Assisi, 'Go into the
> world and proclaim the gospel. Use words if you
> have to.'

To encourage engagement with St. Francis' message, I covered up 'words' in the quotation -

GO INTO THE WORLD AND PROCLAIM THE GOSPEL.
USE _____ IF YOU HAVE TO.

I asked if anyone could guess what the missing word was. There was a deep silence. Then one of the churchwardens attempted an answer. 'Is it "force"?'

GO INTO THE WORLD AND PROCLAIM THE GOSPEL
USE FORCE IF YOU HAVE TO.

As I recount that incident, people usually laugh heartily. At the time I was more saddened than amused. The answer of the mature and able Christian seemed to betray a profound caricature of evangelism which has been a stumbling block to many - within and outside the church. The most notable example in church history of 'evangelism' by force is the Crusades, and they have stained Christian relations with Muslim and Jew ever since. We have to repent of what has sometimes been undertaken by our brothers and sisters in the name of Christ and seek a better way. Jesus provides us with that way.[18]

After all, they say 'honesty is the best policy', so as Christians, let's be honest. People today aren't 'turned on' by the false Christian permanently smiling face.

[18] John Holmes, *Vulnerable Evangelism: The Way of Jesus*, Grove Books Ltd - Ev 54, p.4

Let's admit that:

> life isn't always a bed of roses for Christians;
> I get down sometimes;
> Sometimes I feel like chucking it in!

But through it all, prayer gives me perspective, the Bible gives me guidance, the Holy Spirit gives me strength.

'Vulnerable evangelism' - this is our starting point; this rugged, more honest sharing will at least make more sense to our post-modern, post-Christendom society, who are very sceptical about false religiosity and 'churchianity'.

Learning from Jesus

The disciples wanted to use force too
- against the Samaritans!
Luke 9:51-56

Jesus said: 'You do not know what spirit you are of.'

What did he mean then?

What does it mean for us?

Getting Real in Kelso

As an Adviser in Mission and Evangelism, I'm often invited to
a Kirk Session meeting to begin to open up some of the issues
around mission, working together and healthy church analysis.

On one occasion, I was invited to look at some of the issues
arising out of the "Church Without Walls' report, and at the
dinner table in the manse with the minister just before the
meeting, I was sounding off on what a healthy church should
look like.

I happened to mention that my wife and I had found it difficult
to get involved in a local church when I left the parish ministry
and took up this post. None of my kids goes to church, though
I think they believe in God. Sometimes I end up having to go
to church on my own and I am experiencing just how awkward
that can be. It sometimes breaks my heart - the thing that
means most to me in life isn't a major part of life for my family. I
can't even pass on the good news to my own kids, never mind
anyone else.

I was beginning to feel worse and worse about my job and the
meeting coming up. Then the minister said, 'Share that with
them, David. My elders will be able to identify with what you've
just said.'

And sure enough, although we all got quite excited and
motivated about the thought of working out what it meant to
be a 'church without walls' in that Borders town, perhaps the
most significant communicating took place when I just shared
my story. Heads were nodding in agreement. I realised that it's
never going to be easy to find the best way of sharing the good
news, but it's best to start from our weakness and our humanity,
not from our position of power and not with our religiosity.

Second Conversion

Believe you me, when God called me to the parish ministry, he knew what he was doing! Mind you, it was the last thing I wanted to do - I felt it was ministers that were holding the church back! And yet I could see a certain logic in it - by that time, I had bags of experience in Crusaders, Seaside Mission, leading the Bible class and the youth fellowship; I had preached at an evening service, and I hadn't been long married before I was asked for the second time in my mid-twenties if I would consider the call to the eldership. The folk of Moncreiff Church in Calderwood, East Kilbride (my home church at the time where my mum and brother and his wife are still members) encouraged me to consider the ministry.

So I accepted the call to East Kilbride West Kirk and initially we had to work through some fairly significant issues until we were eventually seeing some growth. I was working in that congregation with some of the finest Christian folk you're ever likely to meet.

And right there, just when I thought that I was getting the family and the church and the world all sorted out, I had the feet taken from under me.

It took a while for my dad, my brother and me to see it but eventually we had to admit that my mother had become an alcoholic. It was months later that, thank God, she herself admitted it to her GP, and then to us; and (one day at a time) she continues to be a recovered alcoholic. But just to share this at appropriate occasions (my mum has given me permission to break her anonymity) builds such bridges of recognition and identification, especially in parts of Scotland (all over?) where drink is a major problem.

My first conversion took place in my late teens when, at an SU (Scripture Union) rally in Clarkston Halls, after the Heralds had made their 'altar call', I prayed that God would come into my life in a meaningful way through the power and presence of his Holy Spirit as I accepted Jesus as my Saviour and Lord.

Then another 'crisis point' occurred in my life which was a kind of conversion back into my humanity and vulnerability. It was literally a crisis of the flesh. I am now grateful to the physician who removed what turned out to be a malignant melanoma (operation: 3/11/92; devastating result: 1/12/92. I keep the dates in my diary the way some of my friends keep the date they became Christians). 'Am I going to die?' 'You can't tell with this, you just have to wait and see. You'll go for regular examinations to the Southern General and we'll keep an eye on the main nodal points. If there's no recurrence after 5 years, things should be OK.' I went home and my wife just held me as I wept.

Then a third crisis eventually overtook me. I was unaware that I still hadn't really coped with the emotions which had been stirred up by the experience of having cancer. The feelings resurfaced a few years later when relationship problems and the normal ups and downs of ordinary married family life heightened my feelings of insecurity. The spell of depression which followed was the darkest experience of my life.

I felt I had truly joined the human race - where 1 in 3 in Scotland will suffer from some kind of cancer and 1 in 5 will suffer from depression at some point in their lives. Of course I had questions. Of course I had doubts about God, love, faith and everything. Sharing the good news at the appropriate time from my position of weakness opened up the way of vulnerability. So remember your humanity. Remember your frailty. Remember the crucified God. There is a mysterious connection between our weakness and God's power.

Robert Warren says on one of the York Courses tapes:

> In the early days, my faith was a celebration of 'Now
> I know the answers.' Now it is the faith that gives me
> the ability to live with the unanswered questions.[19]

Don't you agree that this is what people are looking for today? Of course it is. Most people realise that the problems of living, and suffering, and what lies beyond death are always going to involve mystery. What they want is faith and hope and love to live with the unanswered questions.

> After all, it was out of weakness that the Apostle
> Paul made Christ known:

>> When I came to you brothers and
>> sisters, I did not come proclaiming the
>> mystery of God to you in lofty words or
>> wisdom. For I decided to know nothing
>> among you except Jesus Christ and him
>> crucified. And I came to you in weakness
>> and in fear and in much trembling.
>> 1 Corinthians 2: 1-3 .

---

[19] From a taped interview on *Evangelism Today* published by York Courses.

'Out of the depths, O Lord ...'

What 'body blows' have you suffered during your life?
Where do you feel God was at those times?

If it helps, draw a graph of your life with the ups and downs; or
make a bracelet out of coloured beads with different colours
marking different 'crisis' points.

Where do you see that God was with you?
How does letting people see our vulnerability
make a difference when we share
our faith with others?

Well, there you are Peter, it's about
opening up your life. What does this
way of vulnerability mean to you?

PETER:

Ecclesiastical Agoraphobia

Paul's visit to Corinth rings bells for
me. When I started my ministry in the
centre of Edinburgh in the Parish of St
Cuthbert, I spent the first few weeks
walking the streets and praying for some
wisdom about where to begin in this new
mission field.

.Businesses, theatres, hotels, clubs, restaurants, pubs, tenement flats, homeless people on the streets - this was a new world for me. I was being asked to find ways of relating to the 2,000 people who lived in the area, the 10,000 who worked there, the 20,000 who came through the area at the weekend for entertainment and the significant few who slept in the graveyard.

Out on the streets I had no pulpit from which to preach, no safe church walls where insider language would be understood by insiders, no status of assumed leadership and no expertise or training to equip me for this street-level ministry. I felt naked - and very frightened. I nicknamed my anxiety 'ecclesiastical agoraphobia' - the fear of being in open places beyond the safety of the church!

One night, as I walked and prayed around the clubs and pubs, I remembered words spoken to Paul when he was experiencing cross-cultural angst in Corinth. This former rabbi was out of his depth and he knew it. He was ready to cut and run. Then he had a vision in the night in which God addressed his fears:

> Do not be afraid; keep on speaking and do not be silent, for I am with you. I have many people in this city.[20]

For a moment I was given X-ray vision. I could see through the walls of the offices and the nightclubs. I could see people in their flats or in the graveyard. These were God's people. Some knew it. Most did not. My job was simply to go and find them.

That switch of perspective inside my mind taught me how to come alongside people without any of the trappings of church, to ask questions and to listen. Out of these conversations we found ways of creating space in the business community and the clubbing scene where the Gospel could be shared.

20 Acts 18:9,10 .

59

It meant moving off my safe territory and meeting people where they felt safe, but I felt vulnerable - not unlike those first disciples, sent out on their 'test-run' by Jesus 'like lambs among wolves' without 'purse or bag or sandals'.[21]

He expected minimum resource and maximum courage. It was said of the Celtic missionaries that they had a theology and spirituality of insecurity. That is a challenge to our assumed patterns of evangelism: to dare to move out of our comfort zones and to let go our control of the agenda.

Learning from Jesus

Jesus sent out his squad of seventy with minimum resources.
Luke 10:1-11

What resources do we actually need for sharing the gospel?

Men Only

Long before my escapades on Lothian Road, I had discovered the need to be vulnerable in sharing the gospel. Henri Nouwen described the current requirement for ministry: to be an 'articulator of inner events'.[22]

In a culture of confusion, depression, anxiety and rage, where identity and purpose have been sold out to the latest logo or soap opera, people need Christians who can share the gospel in personal terms.

21 Luke 10:3,4
22 Nouwen, Henri J M, *The Wounded Healer,* Image Books, 1979, p 38

The Christian leader is 'the first to enter the promised but dangerous land, the first to tell those who are afraid what he has seen, heard and touched.' [23]

For a number of years, I led a 'men only' group. Men were invited who had friends or family in the church but who were themselves not Christians. The first gathering was based on the simple question: 'Jesus began with 12 men. Today, few men find church relevant or attractive. Why?'

This approach is not for those of a nervous disposition. The key is to ask the question and let people throw their assumptions, criticisms, prejudices and legitimate complaints at you, and to say nothing in response. It may be your first experience of verbal crucifixion, but the important posture is one of listening deeply.

At the end of the first evening, people were asked if they would appreciate another meeting in three months' time. They replied that they would. And so every three months, the group gathered. A question was thrown into the ring and the issues were thrashed out in an exciting heresy hunt. Over time, relationships moved from the aggressive (usually tempered with good humour!) to honest enquiry, until one by one they started to ask if they could find out more.

Some would come to church for a few weeks and then return to the group to comment on what they had found - or not found. Some would move to a more focused group where the gospel was being explored more explicitly. At their own pace, many of them moved across the stepping stones towards a living faith in Christ.

[23] *Ibid* p 38

Agnostics Anonymous

Another example of the vulnerable approach to evangelism was during a mission in Northern Ireland where, for a week, a group of people met for an hour each day, for a session of 'Agnostics Anonymous'.

The introductions are simple. 'I am Peter, and I am agnostic about the mystery of suffering...' 'I am Sue and I am agnostic about the reliability of the Bible...' 'I am Tom and I am agnostic about the place of Christianity among the world faiths...'

The flip chart fills up with the questions. They are drawing up the agenda for the week. Perhaps for the first time they are being allowed to air their questions and doubts. It may not be new to you, but it is a first time for them and each questioner must be treated with that respect.

We introduce the words of Alistair McGrath that 'Doubt is an invitation to faith.' We take as one fixed point the words of Jesus, 'He that has seen me has seen the Father.' And the journey begins!

By the end of the week, we share the story of questioning Thomas, whose doubts were the expression of the pain and anger of a broken heart rather than the cold calculating questions of the cynic. We suggest that it was not Thomas who needed to touch the wounded hands of Jesus, so much as the wounded hands of Jesus that needed to touch the wounded heart of Thomas.

A cross is set up on the floor. There is music and an opportunity for people to make a response by laying a pebble beside the cross. One by one, they place pebbles round the cross to signify that they are offering their lives to Christ, with all their doubts and questions represented by the pebbles. They have moved to the place where Thomas was, to whisper, 'My Lord and my God!'

The way of vulnerability is the way of honesty - the way of authenticity. People need to see that we are real and that our God is part of our real life with its questions and its mysteries.

Like Paul, we can point to the Cross of Jesus Christ as the final clue to the mysteries of life, but we do so with fear and trembling.

Learning from Jesus

Take time to listen to our question spoken on the Cross.
Mark 15:33-34

How comforting is it to know that, in the midst of his suffering, Jesus did not give an answer, but asked the same question?

Opening the Doors

Incidentally, some of you will be wondering how we created space for the homeless people on our doorstep in Edinburgh. It began by chatting with the guys in the graveyard and asking, 'What would you like the church to do for you?'

'That's easy! Instead of letting us sleep outside, let us sleep inside!'

That was the beginning of our joining with several churches in opening our doors to rough sleepers during the months of December to March, in association with one of the Christian homeless charities. For a few months, the doors stood open to people who usually sat outside. For a few days we became vulnerable.

It is so obvious really. What does the good news of Jesus look like to a homeless man? It tastes and smells like a meal, a bed and a hot breakfast… wrapped up in the ministry of hospitality. Perhaps in those gestures of kindness, our man from the graveyard caught a glimpse of the hospitable God of grace. We certainly did.

5. The Way of Hospitality

'Hospitality means…the creation of a free space
where the stranger can enter and become a friend
instead of an enemy.
Hospitality is not to change people
but to offer them space where change can take place.'

Henri Nouwen [24]

---

[24] Nouwen, Henri J M, *Reaching Out - The Three Movements of the Spiritual Life*, Fount, 1987, pp 68-9

Peter

The Hospitality of God

A young Arts student wandered into
the lecture room of a well-known
theologian just to fill a slot in his course.
He understood very little of what the
theologian said, but he was fascinated.
The lecturer seemed to be enjoying himself - an unusual feature
in itself. But there was more. He was inviting people to share in
the hospitality of God - a God who in Jesus Christ had opened
up the way to come home to the heart of God. For the student
that was the beginning of a journey which led to a living faith in
Jesus Christ. He told the story as part of his funeral tribute to
the lecturer.

Hospitality is at the heart of the good news of the Christian
gospel because it is at the heart of God. Sharing the good news
begins with that same open attitude of hospitality to others -
offering the space where a stranger to God's love may become
a friend of God.

Henri Nouwen, a Dutch Roman Catholic writer on spirituality,
suggests that Christian witness is like inviting a guest into your
house.[25] The guest looks around. He sees pictures on the wall,
music in the CD rack, books on the shelves, the furnishings and
layout of the room. The silent room tells a story of who you are,
before you say a word.

However, if the guest is left in the room alone for too long, the
guest begins to be anxious. The guest speculates and imagines
what you are like, until you enter the room and begin an honest
conversation about your life, family, opinions and beliefs. The
hospitality of the open space is matched by the honesty of open
dialogue.

25 *Ibid* p 92

The hospitality allows the stranger space to be himself. The honesty is the space to be ourselves. As we are honest about who we are in Christ, Christ makes himself known in the space that has been created by the hospitality.

Hospitality through the Ages

Hospitality was treasured in ancient cultures. Jews and Christians spoke of hospitality to strangers as 'entertaining angels unawares'.[26] The Old Testament is full of stories of the significance of welcoming strangers - most famously, Abraham and Sarah entertaining the angel of the Lord who promised them a son in their old age, causing Sarah to burst out laughing in disbelief [27] - and later, the kindness of the penniless widow of Zarephath to the prophet Elijah, resulting in her having enough to feed herself and her son till the drought was over.[28]

In the New Testament, Jesus is always being welcomed into people's homes with all the blessings that come from his healing and disturbing presence. It was Barnabas' generosity of heart that opened the doors to the newly converted Saul of Tarsus, recently a persecutor of the Way.[29] One handshake of hospitality changed the course of history. Later, when Paul was struggling with his future ministry, it was the hospitality of Aquila and Priscilla that gave him a strategic job as a leather-worker, buying hides from the farmers from the country and selling his wares to the affluent upper classes of the city.[30] The effects of the ministry of hospitality are incalculable.

Hospitality was a feature of the Celtic Church. Cuthbert was Guestmaster at the Monastery in Ripon. One cold winter's night, when a young man appeared at the door, Cuthbert took him in and warmed his feet. When Cuthbert went to prepare a meal for the stranger, he returned to find the man had disappeared.

26 Hebrews 13:2;
27 Genesis 18;
28 I Kings 17;
29 Acts 9:27;
30 Acts 18

Mysteriously, there were no footprints in the snow. The story grew into a legend that an angel had visited that night - a legend which enhanced the role of hospitality.

A Celtic monastery always had a room called the 'hospitium' - a room set aside for the guest - and it was always the best room in the house. At the monastery of David in Pembrokeshire, the monks would live on very simple fare, but cook sumptuous meals for the guests.[31] Hospitality meant the best for the stranger - even if that stranger was a criminal on the run or a political exile. The Christian tradition of hospitality is rugged, not romantic!

Our paranoid, security-conscious culture has lost the naturalness of hospitality. Our default position is one of hostility and suspicion -' stranger spells danger'. It is counter-cultural to open our homes to strangers to represent the hospitable God of grace.

I knew a man who had a unique way of sharing his faith. If anyone asked him questions or challenged his faith in Christ, he invited them to come and spend two weeks in his home. He promised never to speak to them about his faith during that time. They were simply to observe his home life. If they saw something worthwhile, they could ask all the questions they wanted. If not, then there was nothing worth saying! Many people took up his invitation and, through his hospitality, discovered the hospitality of God.

Come on, David, don't you have another story to share with us...?

31 Bradley, Ian, *Colonies of Heaven: Celtic Christian Communities*, Northstone Publishing, 2000, p 12

David

Up Close and Personal

Right, Peter. Like most other folk, we're not brilliant at this, but there have been a few special incidents, and this is one of them.

Gwen and I had been married for about five years when, one year into my life as a student minister, I found myself working with another church in East Kilbride (Claremont Parish Church). We had two of our kids at that stage and the house we were in afforded us a spare bedroom-cum-dining room.

But it was still a thought when my 'boss' at that time (the minister of Claremont Church) asked if we could put up a young lad for a while. He was in his teens, had a bit of a drink problem, had had an argument with his dad and was sleeping rough in bin shelters. He needed somewhere to go till he got himself sorted out. So we agreed to meet him and decided we should offer him food and shelter for a while.

I would never now recommend that you take on something like that without first giving it very serious consideration. You see, a family (my family!) is a very fragile thing at the best of times and this just brought in other complications.

Oh, he was great with our kids - they loved having a 'big brother'. But he smoked: we didn't. He wanted to watch telly when we didn't. We went to bed shortly after the kids.were down. He was often in late and wakened us up because we weren't used

70

to having teenagers. He saw us at our best and he saw us at our worst. After a few arguments, we came to some kind of agreement about most of the issues and several weeks down the road, he managed to get a place in the young persons' homeless unit and we parted with some relief (on both sides no doubt!). But that's not the end of the story...

I'm not very good at cleaning the windows as often as I should. We'd been in our most recent house in Lindsayfield, East Kilbride almost two years and I had managed to do the outsides once or twice, but they must have been dirty (again!). Anyway my wife was right onto it when we came back from the shops one Saturday morning and spotted the 'professionals' working their way down our street.

'There's the window cleaner there', she hinted. 'I'll go over and see if he can fit us in,' I replied. I parked the car and wandered over.
'Hi there, could you manage No. 21 as well?' 'Yeah, I'll come over after this.'
It's a great feeling getting your windows done, so as he got to the end of the job I was quite happy to go to the front door and stood with my wallet open.
'That's brilliant. How much do I owe you?'
'Are you thinking of getting them done on a regular basis?'
(Was there a discount for 'regulars' I wondered?)
'No, to be honest, I usually have a go at them myself, so I'll just square up with you.' 'No, it's a' right, don't bother this time, honestly.'

'No, no, you're kidding, I'll have to give you something!'
'No, it's OK. I owe you a lot more than that, David.'

It was just then I recognised him - a bit older (more than twenty years on!) and a little bit greyer, but still the same cheeky smile.

'Jim (not Jim, but that'll do), it's great to see you. Come in and I'll call Gwen. She'd love to see you.'

We got out the old photos of him with his girlfriend and our kids. He shared that he'd been divorced and was about to get married again to a lovely lassie. And I decided I was definitely going to get my windows done again!

So there you are, Peter. If Gwen ever throws me out, I hope you and Dorothy would do the same for this scallywag!

Peter

Creating that Open Space

Not many of us would be able - or willing - for that kind of open door policy, but we can go some way to offering that hospitable space for discovering the love of God.

'Food' is a key word in Christian communication today. Alpha suppers give people space to talk. Ladies' supper/lunch clubs have pioneered the way for years. Men's breakfasts are popular on Saturday mornings. Business lunches are places to connect work and faith. Safari suppers are great for meeting new people and sharing stories of personal faith journeys at each 'watering hole'.

Table-talk in a home, in a pub or cafe follows the example of Jesus who seemed to do much of his good-newsing over meals – in the home of a leper, an income tax collector, a religious leader – or on a hillside. People always came away changed in some way.

In our multicultural society, one of the best ways of increasing mutual understanding of different faiths is around the different festivals where food and hospitality create that space for honest conversation about Jesus Christ and the other world faiths.

In university cities, churches offering hospitality to overseas students have been greatly enriched. For some international students, that is the first contact with Christianity. It may be the first step on their journey to faith in Christ.

Learning from Jesus

Read the account of Jesus' business lunch with Levi.
Mark 2:13-17

What does this teach us about hospitality as one of Jesus' ways of relating to people?

Consider other meals that Jesus shared, and the people involved.

What would it mean for us to follow Jesus in the way of hospitality?

A Warm Welcome?

Willowcreek Community Church in Chicago has become famous for its focus on being 'church for the unchurched'. One of the lessons we can learn from this is to be more sensitive to the needs of people who do not usually attend church, but may be looking for something more.

One Sunday evening, I was visiting a church which had a beautiful foyer where people gathered before the service. I happened to notice a young couple coming to the door. The elders welcomed them very warmly and pointed them towards the sanctuary door. Nervously they edged their way through the 'friendly' crowd who were deeply involved in their conversations. At the door into the church, another elder smiled and handed them a hymnbook.

As they disappeared into the sanctuary, it struck me that there was nobody else in there. They were obviously new. They were in there alone. I made my way through the knots of people, went into the church and sat beside them. I soon learned they were here to meet the minister and ask him to marry them. It was their first time in church.

I sat through the service looking at it through their eyes and listening through their ears! It spoiled a perfectly good service! I would have enjoyed it, but I could feel their discomfort. Hymnbooks, insider prayer language, obscure Bible passages, tacit rules about standing and sitting or singing were strange to them.

Try it someday. Begin with a slow walk up to the church door. What are the physical messages of the frontage? How do people greet you when you enter? What helps you feel at home? What makes you feel like a stranger? Who speaks to you? Who ignores you? In the terminology of Willowcreek, what aspects of the worship are 'seeker-hostile' or 'seeker-friendly'? Is there any indication that we are 'seeker targeted'?.

One friend attended several churches before anyone spoke to him apart from the minister or duty elder. Where was the spirit of hospitality? Hotels often employ 'mystery guests' to go and spend time in their hotels and make assessments of the service, the cleanliness, the catering and other facilities. These reports help hotels to improve their standards of service. Perhaps we should assess our own churches in this way. (You might like to look at a website where someone does do this - the Mystery Worshipper page of www.shipoffools.com, the online magazine of 'Christian unrest'!)

One theatre manager trained his front-of-house staff to ensure that the patrons were given a total theatre experience. It was not only the stage show which would make or mar the evening. It was the atmosphere created by the girls on the door or the man in the box office.

Do we recognise people with the gift of hospitality? They are the people who should be part of the welcome team as people come to worship. The old-style rota where every elder has to do door duty misses the point. Hospitable people create a spirit of hospitality. People who are 'on duty' may convey a very different impression!

And the people on the welcome team should look like the people you want to reach. I was welcomed at a church door recently by a young couple dressed 'smart-casual', with a babe in arms and a toddler on tow. It was not surprising to walk in and find the church filled with young families.

We never have a second chance to make a first impression! .

Tho God of Hoɛpitality

Hospitality will overflow from people who know the hospitality of the grace of God. That was the experience of the young student, mentioned on page 67, and the university lecturer. It is important to recognise the spiritual roots of this openness because the hospitality of grace stretches our boundaries of welcome to include people 'not like us'.

When Jesus was criticised for giving and receiving hospitality among the wrong kind of people, he told the famous story of the prodigal son. Our society is full of people who have opted out of the Father's house and made a mess of their lives. Many feel the shame of that and want to find a way home. When they turn up at our churches will they find the Father's welcome, or elder brother's dismissive comments?

Rob Parsons has written movingly of the need for us to be ready to welcome home the 'prodigals' with acceptance and without judgement. He quotes the prophetic comment of an old man: 'When the Father's house is filled with the Father's love, the prodigals will come home.' [32]

He goes on to describe a group that met in his home called 'The Strugglers' Group', which existed for people in mid-life who had lost their way and wanted to find their way home to God, or people who had burnt themselves out in giving to others so that their own faith was at a low ebb; while others had no faith at all. The group offered a safe haven for a while.[33]

The hospitality of God will stretch our capacity to forgive, to accept and to embrace into the family people whose lives are chaotic and broken. The symbol of our hospitality is not a cup of tea and a biscuit, but a cup of wine and some broken bread.

[32] Parsons, Rob, *Bringing Home the Prodigals*, Hodder and Stoughton, 2003, p 79
[33] *Ibid* p 97-98

Learning from Jesus

*Read the account of Jesus sharing bread with
Judas at the Last Supper.
John 13:21-30*

*Who is your 'Judas' with whom Jesus
wants you to share bread?*

6. The Way of Community

'All the lonely people, where do they all belong?'

from *Eleanor Rigby* (Lennon/McCartney).

DAVID:

It's what this generation is crying out for - community and loving relationships. It's fine having individuals who might be prepared to share the good news, but unless people can see it in action in a group of people caring for one another, then it's worse than useless.

Lesslie Newbigin had the uncanny knack of hitting the nail right on the head -

> How is it possible that the gospel should be credible, that people should come to believe that the power which has the last word in human affairs is represented by a man hanging on a cross? I am suggesting that the only answer, the only hermeneutic of the gospel, is a congregation of men and women who believe it and live by it.[34]

Being Honest about Church

It's not difficult to see what's wrong with the church. So we perhaps agree when someone suggests that in a post-modern world, people might find church a culture shock. We decide to invite friends first of all to a house group or something. Church is the last thing to invite them to. Why do we frequently find ourselves thinking and acting like this? Is it because we're sensitive about the post-modern mindset? No, let's be honest - it's because church is often tedious, irrelevant, embarrassing, old fashioned....

34 Lesslie Newbigin, *The Gospel in a Pluralist Society*, London: SPCK, 1989, p. 227

Graham Tomlin works through lots of these issues in his helpful book, *The Provocative Church:*

> Many Christians are understandably wary of risking a good friendship by inviting someone to what might turn out to be a disastrous and embarrassing event. Yet ... I suspect there is a deeper unease that often prevents Christians from bringing friends to church, and it is this: that in their heart of hearts, *they do not really want to be there themselves*. 'Come and be bored with me' is hardly the best line to attract people to church![35]

From his experience of building a vigorous, growing church, Rick Warren makes the telling point: 'If most of our members never invite anyone to come to our church, what are they saying (by their actions) about the quality of what our church offers?' [36]

In the missionary context in which we live, it is no longer acceptable (was it ever?) simply to gather Sunday by Sunday to sing hymns. In some way, church must be an intimation of the Kingdom of love, peace and justice.

Graham Tomlin again -

> George Monbiot, the author of the influential book *Captive State*, and a key figure in the anti-globalisation movement, describes himself as 'not religious'. Yet he speaks for many when he offers his reasons for drifting away from church: What counts is what churches do, much more than what they profess ...they must match the positive things they say with action.

[35] Graham Tomlin, *The Provocative Church*, SPCK, 2002, p 88
[36] Rick Warren, *The Purpose Driven Church*, Grand Rapids, MI: Zondervan, 1995, p 52.

Unless there is something about church, or Christians, or Christian faith that intrigues, provokes or entices, then all the evangelism in the world will fall on deaf ears … Churches need to become provocative, arresting places which make the searcher, the casual visitor, want to come back for more. …In other words, a community of people that lives by God's ways, that has learnt to place love, humility, compassion, forgiveness and honesty right at the centre will make people think. To put it differently, a church that lives its life under the kingdom of God cannot help but provoke questions. And when it does that, then is the time for evangelism. That is the time for the simple explanation of the good news of Jesus Christ.[37]

Belonging and Believing

PETER:

Belonging comes before believing. The 'Friends' generation looks for a place of acceptance that will embrace them and a community that embodies the faith, hope and love of the gospel.

The Church on the Other Side by Brian McLaren is one person's alarm bell to alert us to the massive changes in our society. He sees us moving through such dramatic changes in our culture that we must begin to lay foundations for 'church on the other side' of the cultural divide.

He sees the challenge of mission as the challenge to create a new kind of Christian community which will begin with 'rawer' material.

37 Graham Tomlin, *The Provocative Church*, SPCK, 2002, pp. 9, 10, 11 & 14 .

The challenge will be to take good middle-class dentists and accountants and help them to emerge from their suburban cocoons to care for their neighbours including their unwashed blue-collar or urban-refugee neighbours in Jesus' name. The challenge will be to get black folk who resent whites and white folk who resent blacks to come together as brothers and sisters who see their humble, barrier-bridging friendships as a form of quiet powerful revolution.[38]

McLaren's book is a revision of an earlier edition which he critiques because he had failed to recognise the importance of 'authentic community' as the basis of evangelism. He confesses that, until recently, he had thought that we simply need 'more Christians and better Christians', individuals following Christ. That approach is the product of an individualism which is neither true to the gospel, nor appropriate for the post-modern culture.

This community will not be inward looking, but will be committed to working for the good of the world. The most evangelistic poster outside a church may state: we believe in a God who does not want children to die - and we are doing something about it.

Many people want to create a better world. They will associate with people who want a better world. Supporting campaigns for clean water, reducing the impact of AIDS, caring for folks with dementia, cleaning up the local riverbank - these are all invitations to share in a Christian community that makes a difference because we believe in a God who makes all things new.

Recent city-wide evangelistic youth missions in London, Manchester and Glasgow have included major social action projects such as cleaning up neglected areas, redecorating homes, digging gardens or building play areas. This has involved young people in down-to-earth service for the community, which lets people know that God is concerned about the whole of life.

38 McLaren, Brian D, *The Church on the Other Side - Doing Ministry in the Post-modern Matrix*, Zondervan, 2000, p 32

The '24/7' prayer movement has mobilised thousands of young people to engage in prayer for cities around the world and, in particular, to send teams to the 18-30 clubbing holiday islands such as Ibiza. As part of their commitment to care and pray for people, they have asked government permission to clean up the beaches following the all-night parties.

The Christian message is about offering wholeness in Christ to the whole person in the midst of the whole of life. To evangelise is to initiate a person into the kingdom of God. These actions may be their first glimpse of the way God wants things to be. People find God by being apprenticed to a community that serves God.

John's Gospel and letters spell out the connection between the God of love and the need for a community of love to make God known. We cannot claim to love God whom we have not seen if we do not love our brother and sister whom we can see. God came in the human flesh and blood of Jesus of Nazareth. Today God needs our flesh and blood to touch our earth and times.

'By this shall all people know that you are my disciples, because you love one another.' (John 13:34) That is the ultimate test - not the correctness of our doctrine, but the quality of our life together.

Belonging that Challenges

Someone once said that 'it makes no difference what you believe if what you believe makes no difference'. That moral challenge is the difference between the kind of spirituality which is about 'me-feeling-good- now' and the spirituality marked by the cross of Jesus Christ. Belonging that leads to believing must also offer a community where our behaviour is transformed.

John Wesley's impact on England in the eighteenth century consisted not so much in his open air preaching, radical and powerful as that was. The thing that brought about lasting change in society was the way he channelled his converts into regular teaching groups where they were held accountable week by week for living life as Christians with consistency.

In a post modern society where commitment is often short-lived and promises are hard to keep, we need to offer patterns of belonging that give us the right blend of support and accountability. It is this that helps us to change to be more like Jesus Christ.

Covenanted Clusters are a simple place to start. It takes no organisation apart from three people agreeing to meet. For several years, I have met with two Christian businessmen every two weeks. We meet at lunchtime in an office in the centre of Edinburgh. We come from our busy mornings and 'splurge' whatever is on our minds. We may talk business ethics or about issues of corporate culture. We talk about family issues or developments in our churches. We have supported each other through various crises, major decisions and transitions in life. We have tried to be honest with each other in ways that have helped us towards a more integrated spirituality. We trust that Christ makes himself known to others through that authenticity.

Learning from Jesus

Jesus gives a very simple image of church
- where two or three gather.
(See Matthew 18: 15-20)
How does this kind of fellowship help
the spread of the gospel?

The Cell-church has been one response to this hunger for community. The phrase 'cell church' reflects the organic quality of every cell in the human body as a life-giving unit which reproduces itself. People meet together in small groups of 6 to 10, under the guidance of two trained leaders. Every cell is expected to fulfil four key functions: welcome, worship, word and witness. As part of the cell, newcomers are exposed to the reality of Christian experience and given the opportunity to grow into faith in Christ. The same cells become the base for nurturing disciples and emerging leaders. This is high-commitment community which is gathered up into regular celebrations as the cells come together in shared worship.

The Iona Community has been built on a commitment of people to live with an open accountability to each other - to pray, to use money wisely and work for a better world. In a society which struggles with commitment, we need people who will express the image of a God who makes promises and keeps them. People sometimes find that they cannot commit themselves to anything. Their ability to trust has been eroded because they have been betrayed once too often. Helping people have faith for life takes time.

The Corrymeela Community in Northern Ireland has been a sign of reconciliation for decades in a country divided by religious and political hatred. The community stands as a challenge to every church today to be a sign of reconciliation in a broken world. The hallmark of Christian community is forgiveness. The hallmark of our society from family to politics is conflict. The biggest challenge in communicating the gospel of forgiveness lies in creating a community that embodies it - where people can see a role model of conflict resolution and reconciliation. The message of the cross is best heard from among 'friends of the crucified',[39] where the marks of the cross are visible: service, forgiveness and sacrificial care for one another and the world around.

[39] Nessan, Craig L, *Beyond Maintenance to Mission - a theology of the congregation*, Augsburg Fortress, 1999, p 56.

Learning from Jesus

Read about Jesus' community of forgiveness.
Matthew 18:21-35

What would change in your church if you lived out
this core value of forgiving people?
What areas of your community would change?

What about the children?

So what's new about this assertion that belonging leads to believing -this assertion that is the central affirmation of the covenant community of the baptised?

A church which has practised infant baptism for centuries believes that people come to faith within the household of faith. We affirm the truth of that saying from Africa that 'it takes a whole village to raise a child'. When a child is baptised in the name of the Father, Son and Holy Spirit, the child is welcomed by a relational God into a communal expression of grace to learn a communal faith.

The promise of God, the promises of the parents and the promises of the congregation weave a web of grace around the child within which we promise to enable the church to grow from the crèche up!

The test of the baptismal vows lies in the body language of the church community - in the place that children have in the worship, fellowship and service of the church. Emil Brunner claimed that the church took a false turning when we substituted the classroom for the community of faith as the place of nurture.

That test is even more challenging as churches make space for teenagers or leave them out in the cold. And for those who are fortunate to have young people in church, how well do we prepare them with the life-skills to be Christians at work, college or university? To develop a baptismal community is a life's work.

Sadly, the rich ritual of baptism is not backed by the investment of time, structure or money needed to create that nurturing environment for faith. Statistics tell the story. The numbers of children being baptised or attending church has dropped dramatically in the past 20 years. The losses are seen even more dramatically in the figures for teens, twenties and thirties. The old myth about people leaving in their teens and returning in their thirties is a mirage of false hope.

Learning from Jesus

Children are essential reminders of the Kingdom of God.
Matthew 18:1-6

If we leave children out of the church family,
what will we miss?

There is a great deal of work being done to help us create more child-friendly and family-friendly churches. This calls for long-term investment that thinks in decades rather than months.

Some churches have members (of the guild or similar group) who pray for every child baptised over a period of years. Other churches invest time in preparing parents for the vows of baptism and offer parenting courses to help them fulfil the vows that they have taken. One church offers a course on

'Motherhood and Theology' to help young mothers think together about God's place in their role of nurturing their children. Another church offers imaginative materials to families during Advent to encourage parents and children to play and pray together in the lead up to Christmas.

The trouble is that this focus - which is vital - is on children who are in Christian families or who are already associated with the church in some way. This is a rapidly diminishing market. According to the UK Christian Handbook, the percentage of the UK child population in Sunday Schools dropped dramatically during the course of the 20 th century - from 55% in 1900 to 4% in 2000. [40]

The issue may be that we are looking in the wrong direction. Sunday contact is no longer the measure of our success. Children are associated with the church through other agencies and organisations during the week, from uniformed organisations to breakfast clubs and after school clubs - including one village after-school café called 'Sunday School on Wednesday'! Thus in Scotland, the churches are in touch with 102,000 young people under 25 through these midweek church activities. This, however, represents only 6.6% of the population under 25 - and of that number, only 14% will be in church on Sunday.[41]

That is why, in order to win the rising generation, we will need to 'stop starting with the church', and recover appropriate patterns of evangelism among children and young people. George Barna's research in the USA, working with a sample of 4,000 people, suggested that 'if people do not make a commitment to Christ by the age of fourteen, the likelihood of ever doing so is slim.' [42]

[40] UK Christian Handbook, Religious Trends No 2, 2000/1, quoted in *Mission-Shaped Church*, Church House Publishing, 2004 p 41
[41] Brierley, Peter, *Turning the Tide: The Challenge Ahead - Report of the 2002 Scottish Church Census*, Christian Research, 2003
[42] Booker, Mike and Ireland, Mark, *Evangelism - Which Way Now?*, Church House Publishing, 2003, p 107 .

While not agreeing to cage the God of grace in that kind of sociological determinism, the facts remind us that there is a massive task in befriending, mentoring and discipling two (and maybe three) generations that are beyond earshot of church-based communication of the gospel.

One church in an Urban Priority Area on the edge of Perth is asking this question: 'How do we take second and third generation non-Christian children and young people and help them to be consistent followers of Jesus Christ in today's world?'

This church works with excluded youngsters in the schools. They offer a range of youth activities including sport. They take the youngsters away for weekend events. They currently have a queue waiting for their Christian discipleship class. Older and younger people are involved in the activities so that if the young people arrive at worship on Sunday, they recognise people of all ages. In the past three years, some 40 young people have come to faith in Christ.

This is costly work. Phone calls at night or early in the morning tell of youngsters evicted from their homes. They have to live up to their strapline of being a 'wounded incarnate community'. All the challenges of being a hospitable community are met here in an earthy way.

In these tragic days of domestic abuse to women and children, we need to be ready to face the raw issues of broken lives and broken trust. Professor Bob Holman of Easterhouse has called for churches to become 'family centres' which are not only responding to family problems, but creating a community where people who have had no healthy role models find good patterns to follow.

This evangelism business becomes more and more complex. As an African Christian put it: 'Evangelism is like ivory hunting. You find a tusk and discover there is an elephant attached!'

The Hub Church

Today's society is a network society. People may not know their neighbours next door, but they find their community at work, at the sports centre or at the pub. If we are to offer Christian community for people to come to faith in Christ, then we will need to meet people where they are…and stay there! The church that wants to make Christ known will become a network of dispersed communities that follow Christ in his journey of Incarnation:

"The Word became a human being and moved into the neighbourhood." John 1:14 [43]

This approach is not new. It is the way these islands were evangelised in the beginning. The Celtic Church developed their monasteries as places of the 'heart, home and hub' - nurturing hearts for God, offering a home to friend and stranger, and becoming a hub which equipped people to travel to meet people where they were. Much of this would be at the wells - the places of local community and spirituality. That is where they preached and baptised people.

The spiritual seekers today look for our Christian churches to be that place of the 'heart' - either in celebration or in quiet reflection. Many test us by the warmth of our welcome and hospitality.

However, most will never come near our church buildings. Our churches must become that 'hub' that sends us out to meet people at the 21 st century 'wells' where people meet together in our communities. For some that will be the local pub or club, the gym or the line dancing, the snooker or the football, the housing association or the local centre for homeless people.

43 Peterson Eugene H, *The Message*, Navpress, 1995 .

Shaping Church to the Contours of Life

St Thomas's is located to the north of Sheffield in a clutch of industrial units in an old industrial estate. These units offer worship space for 1,200 people, office accommodation, an online shop, a chapel and a training centre. The central buildings are about to be demolished to create a day-care nursery, an arts centre, a chapel for 100 people and a piazza which will form a centre to the campus - known as Philadelphia because of the promise of Christ to hold before us 'an open door'.

This thriving church is set in a city which has 2% of its population attending church and which is on the way to becoming the youngest city in Britain. The church's focus has been to minister among Generation X.[44] The ministry of Mike Breen over the last ten years has built on 27 years of the outstanding work of Robert Warren. This is the fruit of 40 years of ministry - and more.

The Sheffield church takes account of the contours of everyday life for this generation: working through networks for pastoral support and evangelism, relating to people where they are in work or through football teams or night clubs. People are encouraged to discover their 'life skills' as a basis of Christian living in today's society. Small cell groups or 'huddles' offer a space for accountability as in the model of Wesley. These cell groups are formed into clusters of 40 to 50, designed to represent our need for extended family for rounded growth. The celebrations are formed by clusters coming together for worship around their missional intentions. The Sunday evening gatherings are for teaching for the cluster leaders - 45 minutes' worship, 30 minutes' tea break and 45 minutes' teaching - with the option to come to any one of the segments.

[44] 'Generation X' is the name given to the cohort in society born between 1964-81. They are sometimes called 'busters' because they have lived through the 'bust-up' of family life. Bill Wilson, *Streets of Pain* Authentic Lifestyle, STL .

Here is the clue and the challenge to Christian community for a post modern age: church follows the basic contours of our humanity rather than forcing our humanity into predetermined contours of church structure.

In that place of belonging, Christian believing and behaving follow on.

7. The Way of Discovery

'We live at a time when the Church of tomorrow is and should be coming to birth alongside the church of today… The last few years have been an almost unprecedented period of Christian creativity.' 45
Mike Booker and Mark Ireland

45 Booker and Ireland, op cit p 186

DAVID

Models in the Marketplace

Evangelism - which way now? by Mike Booker
and Mark Ireland is an excellent survey
of the many approaches to evangelism
that have emerged in the UK in recent
years. The authors survey the *Alpha*
Course, the *Emmaus* Course, *Christianity
Explored, Essence* and the *Y* course,
as well as broader themes of cell
church, community ministry, children's
evangelism and church planting.

A look at the table of contents reminds us that for those who
want to be engaged in sharing the Christian faith today in ways
that are authentic and effective, there are many models to guide
us. Where there is a will there are many ways!

In the preface to their book, Booker and Ireland make a number
of significant summary statements:

- there is no single answer to the question in the title
- there are some excellent tools to choose from
- small successes are worth celebrating
- God is full of surprises… we celebrate a missionary God
  who is already active in the world
- evangelism is worth it…Jesus has encouraged us to
  share the good news with abandon, knowing that
  where it does bear fruit, the harvest will be out of all
  proportion to the seed sown 46.

46 Booker and Ireland, op cit pp xi, xii

The range of models is very helpful. Most of us are adaptors rather than innovators, and we encourage people to work with any of these approaches and tailor them to the local situation and to the ethos of their local church. Remember! - the longest journey begins with a single step.

Tracing Shifts in Evangelism

These practical models reflect principles and patterns that have been developed to meet the needs of our times. After years of research leading up to and including what was known as 'The Decade of Evangelism' (the 1990's), Robert Warren detected important shifts in our understanding and practice of evangelism. We use his material here with permission.[47]

There are several discernible shifts in the way the church is doing evangelism today. This is not so much a conscious, co-ordinated change, and certainly not centrally directed; it is rather the natural response of a healthy body to a changed environment. Set out as they are below, in contrasting pairs of ideas, these trends should not be seen as an abandoning of the first idea in favour of the second; but rather the re-working of the more familiar first idea from the standpoint of the second.

From Event to Process

This is the biggest shift to emerge out of the Decade of Evangelism. It is a shift from seeing the normal context of evangelism as happening at a single meeting, event or contact to one of 'accompanying people on the journey of faith'. This has been given greatest visible expression in the widespread use of courses such as *Alpha, Emmaus* and *Christianity Explored,* as well as in the emergence of many such courses which have been locally developed.

---

47 The description of the shifts is borrowed directly from Robert Warren's seminar materials.

Please note what we are *not* saying here - we are not saying that there is no longer any need for special mission events. The journey to faith is a process, but within that process, one or more crisis points and major steps forward may still be of fundamental importance.

David Banbury, an evangelist working with the Church Pastoral Aid Society, has identified the following advantages of mission events:

" For people inside the church, a mission
• builds up and deepens congregational faith
• creates greater confidence in personal evangelism amongst the congregation
• builds up a sense of unity in the body
• helps to keep mission and evangelism as a key element of church life

For people outside the church, a mission gives people the chance to move on in the Christian journey, including
• becoming interested in spiritual things
• being interested in finding out more and being attracted to process evangelism courses
• making decisions to follow Christ" [48]

From Speaking to Listening

Whereas the starting point has often been simply that of 'telling the good news', what is increasingly happening now is that we find ourselves listening to the context into which we are speaking and to the questions being asked, in order to discern what God is calling us to say in that situation. This is evident in the way Jesus spoke to individuals. He adopted a variety of starting-points because he discerned the way in which the good news would touch the life of the person to whom he was speaking.

[48] Mike Booker and Mark Ireland; *Evangelism - Which Way Now?*, Church House Publishing, 2003, pp. 67 & 68

From Doctrine to Spirituality

Our concern in the past has often been with helping people to hear and know the truth about Jesus Christ, so that they might come to know him personally. But what is actually happening more often today is that people are led into some **experience** of God in Christ - e.g. through the *Alpha* 'Holy Spirit weekend/day' or some other course - as a result of which they are provoked into exploring the truth about the One whom they have encountered. We are in a culture which is suspicious of religion and religious institutions but which is open to the spiritual dimension of life. It's important that we learn to make this our starting point.

From 'Bolt-on' to Bloodstream

Evangelistic activities stuck onto the overactive life of a church may add to its problems rather than add to its numbers. We need to find ways of making the church's life itself 'translucent of the gospel'. Where churches are living and engaging communities of faith, others are drawn to it and to Christ who is the centre of such places. Healthy evangelism functions in the context of a church which is, itself, good news.

From Life-changing to Life-enhancing

The emphasis has shifted from confrontation to transformation, from crisis conversion of faith to on-going conversion to the likeness of Christ. In some ways this contemporary shift is the 'odd one out' because it raises fundamental theological questions, such as the fallen nature of mankind and regeneration; and these matters should be given serious consideration. But this shift also challenges us to think deeply about which way the trend in evangelism should go and what the most helpful starting-points might be today. The gospel has traditionally been seen as a call to obedience, service and self-sacrifice. In today's culture, 'spirituality' is focused much more on the consumer mentality of 'what's in it for me?' As a church we need to consider how we address this (apparent?) conflict. How can we start from the self and yet show that self finds fulfilment in self-giving love to the Other and to others?

From Authority to Authenticity

In the past the gospel has been proclaimed largely on the basis of an appeal to a higher authority - 'The Bible says ...', 'The church says ...' etc. Today, what commends the gospel to our culture is the way of life of people who believe and live by the values of the good news embodied in Christ. This is about living our message - something which is a major challenge, especially for the church in the western world.

Take Your Time!

At the risk of being criticised for not taking seriously enough scriptural imperatives about urgency, let's ease the pressure on churches here a little. We're not necessarily looking for newcomers to arrive spontaneously at the church door and have a 'Damascus Road' experience. While 31% of people do claim a datable experience, most people (69%) come to a living faith in Christ through a gradual process.[49]

John Finney's significant research shows that for someone to move from a point of no interest to becoming a believer can take some time:.'the gradual process is the way in which the majority of people discover God and the average time taken is about four years.' [50]

---

49 John Finney, *Finding Faith Today*, Bible Society, 1992, p. 24.
50 *Ibid*,p.25.

Other research has revealed that the process of coming to faith can take something like **3 years for women and 5 years for men** (everyone knows that men are slow!). It may help to look at this as a 4- level process:

Level 1: There might be no spiritual input at all.
Well, let's be honest, spiritual comments could be a bit scary for the person you're just getting to know. They need time to get to know that you're not a religious nutter, that you book your holidays on the internet, that you have arguments in the family, that you like the occasional fish supper and all that stuff. You might share a hobby - five-aside football, line dancing, fishing, hill-walking.

Level 2: An invitation
One or two years down the road, you might invite your friend to a one-off Christian event - a sports dinner or a ladies' supper club.

Level 3: An opportunity to learn more...
Then it may be appropriate eventually to invite them to a Christian basics course like *Alpha* or *Christianity Explore*d. They've got to know you and they trust you not to 'land them right in it'.

Level 4: Are they interested?
They may then show interest in finding out more about what the church is all about and be incorporated into the church family and discipleship.

In today's climate where people find it very difficult even to go across the door of a church, please note that the first 3 steps will probably be away from church altogether!

Nurtured into Faith

More recent unpublished research by John Finney shows that about one in six of those on nurture courses become adult Christians. Well over a million people have been on one or other of these courses *(Alpha, Christianity Explored, Emmaus* - which one doesn't seem to matter). Over 250,000 new Christians have found faith through these nurture groups, most of whom have gone on to become adult disciples.

We can expect a dip in numbers and excitement in the second and third courses a church runs - but the fourth (and beyond) is the most fruitful evangelistically.

There are several reasons why these nurture groups seem to be so helpful for so many people:

1. They are based on relationships not on distant preaching, or books, or going to church - but on people helping people to find Christ. The nurture group enshrines this principle of 'one beggar telling another beggar where to find bread'. The companionship and mutual support of the group is all-important, and is the most-often mentioned factor in evaluations.

2. People learn and laugh Good nurture groups follow the example of good adult education practice. Adults learn best when they are relaxed, enjoying themselves and have a goal to reach (most do not enjoy just arguing for the sake of it - though my brother-in-law does!). Groups need to be happy and aiming at something together. When that is achieved, finding out about God becomes an exciting mutual exploration.

*3. They are group-based but church-link*ed. A nurture group is not separate from the church: it should be owned by the church, encouraged by the church and part of the church. But it is not a church in its own right - it is a group which aims to bring people into full Christian discipleship, and part of that means being committed to the local church.

4. Faith is seen as either journey or crisis. As we have seen, John Finney's research[51] showed that 69% of adults come to faith gradually, while 31% come to faith suddenly. The majority actually travel 'the Emmaus Road' to faith; the minority go down 'the Damascus Road'. A nurture group should look for both kinds of spiritual awakening.

5. They offer space for testimony and explanations. Postmodernism loves stories, especially stories of what happened to someone. So giving people the chance to tell the story of their lives and how their faith has developed is important. But that is not enough -there has to be explanation of why things happened so that others can learn from your experience. Because we're all a mixture - a bit modernist (liking facts), a bit post-modernist (liking stories) - it is not enough to make it all experiential or to make it only cerebral. We must both experience Christ and learn about him.

6. They are non-manipulative and encourage personal exploration. Some evangelism in the past has rightly been accused of being manipulative and of making people conform to a certain pattern. A nurture group should let each person discover (or not!) at their own pace, without expecting them to tread a predetermined path.

*7. They can meet in non-church surroundings.*This may be best, so that non-churchgoers are not intimidated. A common place is someone's house, but groups have met in pubs, community halls, hotels, nightclubs, or wherever people feel at home.

51 John Finney, *Finding Faith Today*, Bible Society, 1992, p. 24

Learning from Jesus

Jesus spent three years with twelve named people.
Mark 3:13-18

*How far is our weakness in evangelism to the many
related to our reluctance to go deeper with
a few in discipleship?*

The Cycle of Grace

Evangelism grounded in grace

These patterns of sharing the good news are based on
more than the pragmatism that 'it works.' At their best they
invite people into experiencing the grace of God as a deep
acceptance that confronts the profoundly destructive patterns of
human behaviour.

Most of us are living life the wrong way round!

Take a look at this diagram. Start with 'Achievement' and follow
the sequence in an anti-clockwise direction.

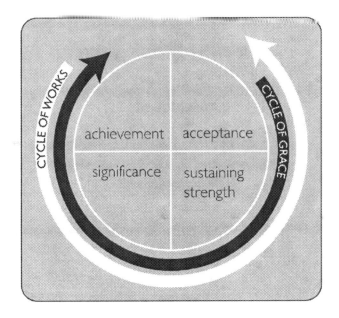

As long as I can keep working for my company, working for my family, working for my church, working for my Lord… just as long as I can keep doing, doing, doing … as long as I'm **achieving** and working, I get my **significance**, this is what gives me **strength**; and so I feel **accepted** by my boss, by my family, by my church, by my God. In this mode we're driven by unhealthy motives of achievement and failure.

The problem is that we get trapped into this wrong cycle - as churches and as individuals. It's addictive, and in the end it is the way of death. It is a self-destructive pattern of living. We're all there at one time or another - workaholics, people-pleasers. When my pal thought I was doing too much at the expense of family, health and everything else, he used to tell me to drive past the local cemetery occasionally - 'It's full of people who thought they were indispensable!'

Take another look at the diagram. Jesus lived the other way round. His starting-point was his **acceptance by God**.
The gospel writers tell us that after John baptised Jesus '… the Holy Spirit came down upon him … like a dove. And a voice came from heaven, "You are my own dear Son. I am pleased with you." …' (Luke 3: 22.) **The Father's acceptance!**

All of Jesus' life thereafter flows from this acceptance. He receives the **sustaining strength** of the Holy Spirit. From his baptism he is led straight into 'the wilderness' for a time of testing and temptation, during which he continues to derive this strength from the Spirit.

When Jesus returns from the desert to Nazareth, he speaks with the conviction that 'the Spirit of the Lord is upon him'. Jesus has discovered a profound sense of purpose and **significance** in fulfilling God's purposes. All his **achievements** - his good works, his acts of kindness, his preaching, his healing, his miracles, everything! - flow ultimately from this.

When we live our lives in a clockwise direction, with Jesus, we are living in the 'cycle of grace'. When we live our lives in an anti-clockwise direction, we live out the 'cycle of works'.

All evangelism is a call to turn away from living by our own efforts to living trusting in the grace of God, in company with Jesus Christ. Through him we know we are accepted in the Father's love. Through him we receive the strengthening power of the Holy Spirit to live for God. Through him we discover our calling and purpose. Through him we are given the grace to take up our cross and follow him through the cross into the resurrection life of Christ.

Wherever we find places and people who embody for us that acceptance of us by God - people who prayerfully help us to be open to the Spirit and invite us to share in God's work in the world - then we have found places for awakening faith in Christ.

In the light of these foundational rhythms of God's grace, it is hardly surprising that nurture groups are a fertile starting point for the post modern seeker, caught up in today's world of performance-related appraisals at work and relational confusion at home.

Personal Reflection

In what ways can you identify with the Cycle of Works in your own journey?
(family, career, etc.)

What would be the effect of learning to live in the other direction?

Spend time meditating on the story of Jesus' baptism.

Imagine Jesus inviting you to join him in the water where you hear the Father's acceptance and receive his Spirit.

Step out of the water with Jesus and join him in his mission.

What does it all mean to you?

The Journey

PETER

Over 30 years of ministry, the place where I have most often seen people come to faith has been through 'nurture groups' based on these practical and theological principles.

As a minister in Glasgow, every Thursday evening was the evening set aside for the 'Enquirers' group'. The group ran continuously throughout the year apart from Christmas and the summer holidays. Over twelve weeks we would discuss the questions that people had about God and suffering, explore some basic themes about the life, death and resurrection of Jesus and introduce people to some of the basic disciplines of prayer and biblical reflection.

When people came about baptisms or weddings, they would be invited to join the group on the following Thursday. Nobody had to wait. It did not matter that they came into the 'middle' of a course. They simply stayed with the group till the themes came round to their starting point. They found acceptance. They found people beginning to pray for God to be present in their lives. They found people wrestling with the call of Christ. They discovered God among people who were discovering God.

It was always a time of surprises as atheists, agnostics and active seekers found that God had found them - even when they were playing hide and seek with God.

More people came to faith through these evenings of honest exploration than through any other approach - be it preaching or special mission events.

Later, in Edinburgh, the course was developed, drawing on some of the *Emmaus* materials, and advertised as *The Journey*.

The meetings were less regular, but the impact was no less effective, as one by one, people came to a living faith in Christ. People who had been associated with the church for many years discovered a reality that had escaped them. People whose lives had been deeply damaged found healing in the love and acceptance of Christ. People who had espoused other faiths for many years were surprised by the God they found in Jesus Christ.

It was Eugene Peterson who joked that Jesus spent three years with twelve Jews in order to win all Americans! We seem to try every other method but miss the one he showed us!

8. The Way of the Story

*'Either our lives become stories or there's
no way to get through them.'*
Douglas Coupland [52].

[52] Coupland, Douglas, *Generation X - Tales for an Accelerated Culture*, Abacus, 2002, p 10

Peter

In *Generation X,* Douglas Coupland tells
the story of three twenty-somethings
who have become bored with life in their
'Mcjobs' and who now live in a bungalow
in Palm Springs in the Californian
desert. One comes from Toronto, one
from Los Angeles and the third from
Oregon, but 'where you come from
feels sort of irrelevant these days'. They
belong to a mobile, rootless generation.

Life has lost any sense of meaning. One of the friends declares
that their lives can only find meaning when they are part of
a story. The three make a pact to contact each other every
evening and tell each other stories - some of them pure fantasy
- that will give their lives some shape.

The three Generation X-ers represent a culture which is often
described as not believing in 'Big Stories' any more. So they
have to invent their own.

For centuries, Western Europe took its meaning from the
Christian story, and shaped its social and political life around a
pattern of customs that we call Christendom; more specifically
in Scotland, the principles of the Protestant Reformation
shaped the nation for 400 years, so that the words 'Scot' and
'Presbyterian' were almost synonyms. We are living through a
period of history where these old categories have disappeared.

Social commentators speak of our society as being post-
Christendom, post-Enlightenment and post-modern. It feels a bit
like driving a car while looking in a rear-view mirror! The mood
of uncertainty tells us that we know where we have been, but
we are not sure where we are going.

Story time

This is the world in which we are to re-tell the story of Jesus. It is a world in which the old certainties have gone and truth claims are suspect. The good news is that, while people reject claims of absolute truth, we are all up for a good story! Like the characters in *Generation X,* people know that we need stories to make sense of life. Ask the millions who watch the TV soaps.

Sharing our faith today is less about making a convincing argument and more about telling an authentic story. People recognise the ring of truth when they hear it. That liberates every one of us into the role of story-telling,

Cold Mountain [53] tells the story of a soldier returning from the American Civil War in search of the young woman he loves. Every person he meets has a story to tell. It becomes an epic tale that gathers into it a dozen small-scale stories of love and war, of goodness and cruelty, but carries in it an unusually pure tone of virtue and dignity. The tale has been likened to Homer's Greek epic poem of Ulysses returning from the battle of Troy and his adventures along the way.

Sharing our faith - and the liberation into story-telling - could be an image of the place of each Christian's story wrapped up in God's larger story revealed in Jesus Christ. Some people are able to tell the bigger story in a way that draws people into it. They are people with the gift of evangelism. Others of us are not so confident about that, but we are able to tell our own story. We tell stories of what we have experienced of God in our lives - what we have witnessed with our own eyes. We are all "witnesses".

53 Frazier, Charles, *Cold Mountain,* Vintage Books, 1998 - now a major motion picture.

*David, I think you have something
to say about telling the story to others.*

David

Yes, Peter, every life
tells a story. And who
knows who's listening?

Throughout the course of an ordinary day, each one of us
makes contact with many different people. Many of these
folk make up our network of family and friends, neighbours,
colleagues, workmates and acquaintances.

Whether we like it or not, we are witnesses to these people. I
think it was Professor Willie Barclay who said, 'It's a sobering
thought to think you might be the nearest thing to Jesus some
people will ever see.' Some of our neighbours and friends might
be weighing up the church and the gospel on the evidence of
our lives.

The Greek word the Bible uses to describe this network of
contacts is *'oikos'*. So who are the people in your *oikos*?

Identifying your oikos

Take a piece of paper and jot down the names of all the people with whom you have regular contact - perhaps those whom you see face to face at least once a fortnight.
Use these categories - family, friends, workmates, neighbours, acquaintances (i.e. people you meet through clubs, hobbies and sports you're involved in).
Mark those who are already Christians.
From the rest, choose two or three people who are uppermost in your mind for one reason or another.
It is hard to witness to your closest friends and family members, so you might want to begin with people who aren't so close.
Write their names, or just their initials for confidentiality, on a card.
This becomes a prayer card for your oikos.

Paul's letter to the Colossians gives us some pointers about what to do next:

Colossians 4:2 - be persistent in prayer

Colossians 4:3 - pray that God will give a good opportunity to share the story of Jesus

Colossians 4:5 - make good use of every opportunity you have

Pray for the people in your *oikos*. Lend them a hand from time to time. Maybe lend them a book or video if they're showing interest, or invite them to the next *Alpha* group.

And remember - just be yourself!

Jesus' last words to his disciples before he left this world were:

> 'But when the Holy Spirit comes upon you, you will
> be filled with power, and you will be witnesses for
> me in Jerusalem, in all Judea and Samaria, and to
> the ends of the earth.' Acts 1:8

Remember - no pressure. Just be yourself! You may be a single parent, a lawyer, a mechanic, a teacher, a canteen worker, an accountant, a cleaner…but whatever you are, wherever you are, you're a witness. That's the whole point. Billy Graham can't be there. Your minister can't be there. The apostle Paul can't be there! Right there, in those positions and jobs, whatever they are, *you* can be - *you* are! - a witness for Jesus Christ.

The Myth of Big Names

There's a nasty rumour going around about the way Christianity spread all over the world. That rumour suggests that it was the 'big names' that brought about the spread of Christianity to different parts of our globe.

Well I'm delighted to be able to say, as I stake a claim for the important part played by ordinary folk like you and me, that in the light of a close examination of the historical evidence, this theory just does not stand up.

Here are three stories that make the point very powerfully. We are grateful to the evangelist John Young for allowing us to use them.

• How did the gospel come to England?

Most of us know that St. Augustine brought Christianity to Canterbury in 597AD. We know this - and we are wrong. In 314AD, English bishops attended the Council of Arles in Gaul. How could this be if we had to wait another 275 years for Augustine of Canterbury? And how can we account for the fact that Augustine was greeted by a Christian Queen?

In fact, Christianity came to these shores shortly after the death and resurrection of Jesus. True, it was pushed to the west (hence 'the Celtic Church') and there was plenty for Augustine and his team to do. The question remains: who first brought the faith to these shores? *The glorious answer is that we don't know.*

The faith came here, not as the result of the preaching of a great evangelist, but in the lives and on the lips of a host of anonymous traders, travellers and sailors. In other words, faith spread through lay people who bore witness to their faith in Jesus Christ.

• How did the gospel reach Rome?

Rome is another example. Surely the church in the capital of the empire was founded by a great missionary saint? Again the glorious answer is *No*. True, Peter and Paul travelled there (and probably died there in or around 64AD). But by the time they arrived, the church was already flourishing. The church in Rome was planted because ordinary Christians - traders and the like - shared their faith and were 'always ready to give a reason for the hope that was in them'. (1 Peter 3:15)

• How has the gospel spread in China?

In modern times, the church in China tells a similar story. Before Chairman Mao took over in 1949, there were about 3 million Chinese Christians.

Then came the cultural revolution. Churches were closed, and pastors were forced to become peasants in a ferocious attempt to extinguish Christianity. Today, the Christian church in China is much larger than in 1949 -estimates vary from 20 million to 80 million and one expert has written of 'Christianity fever'.

How did this happen? Through the witness of the laity. There was no other way possible. The lessons for us are obvious - and crucial.[54]

God uses ordinary people, not just 'the Big Names'.

Learning from Jesus

The risen Jesus revealed himself first to a woman whose word would count for nothing in a Jewish court of law.
John 20: 1-18

How far has the gospel been put on hold by leaving evangelism to specialists?

---

54 John Young, *The Archbishop's School of Evangelism*, York Courses, 2002, p. 7

*Peter, how do ordinary people share
the Christian story today?*

Peter

Christian Conversationalists

We need
good Christian
conversationalists
- people who are at ease in
talking about their faith in a
way that allows others to be at
ease as well. We need people
who are unembarrassed and
unembarrassing.

I have a good friend who simply hangs out with folk and before
you know it, he is talking to them about God and Christ. He will
just as easily invite them to a barbecue or a party or a prayer
group. He is natural, unassuming and non-threatening.

He spent a few weeks recently in a group with people of many
different faiths and none. He found it a disturbing experience,
for he was genuinely open to the challenges that came from the
members of the Baha'i faith or the Hindu faith. He had to take
the criticisms of the church's violent history from the Crusades
to the Inquisition. He was accused of arrogance for his belief in
Jesus as the way to the Father (I cannot think of a more humble
lad!), and generally had to rethink his position in the light of
these questions.

We spent hours talking through these conversations. It helped
to remember that Jesus never said that he was the way to *God*.
He said that he was the only way to the *Father*. Many people
have God-encounters, but the face of that God is only seen as
'Father' in the person of Jesus.

He spent a lot of time with these folks. He prayed a lot and he hung in there with them as friends. After a couple of months, he found that people were coming up to him privately to ask more about his Christian faith. Each one of them had found their foundations shaken by the conversations. He seemed to be the one who had a firm grasp on what God was like. They wanted to know more.

Here is a Christian conversationalist at work. It takes courage and courtesy that are rooted in a humble confidence in Christ.

That same young man is a great traveller. He hitch-hiked recently with a friend from Edinburgh to the south of England. As they travelled, they prayed for opportunities to share their faith with others. Again and again the conversations would open up.

I can just imagine the driver asking the usual questions.
'Where are you going?'
'We are going to a conference on prayer and clubbing.'
'What do you do?'
'I am working out what it means to be a Celtic monk in this culture.'
These are either conversation stoppers or topics to keep them going for miles!

His travelling companion would make an offer.
'Is there anything that we can pray for in your life?'
Nobody refused to share with them a concern about their family or their future. People were happy to believe in people who believed in God. Seeds of the gospel were sown all down the M1!

A Hitchhiker's Guide to Gaza

*Philip hitched a lift on the road to Gaza and touched
the continent of Africa.
(Acts 8:26-40)*

*Do a slow motion re-run of Philip's conversation.
How many tips can you pick up about sharing the gospel?*

E+R+E+R!

That story of the young hitch-hiker seems so like the way in
which Jesus sent his disciples to go and preach and heal in
the expectation of the kingdom of God coming among them. If
we look at the way the gospel spread in the ministry of Jesus
and in the Acts of the Apostles, we can see a pattern which can
be written in a short formula: E+R+E+R = event + reaction +
explanation + response.

Here is an example: Jesus healed a blind man [55]. The
authorities reacted adversely to him and started questioning
the man about Jesus. The man could only give the simplest
explanation: 'I was blind, but now I can see!' Then Jesus made
himself known to the man and invited a response. The man
believed. The religious authorities did not.

In the book of Acts we find the same pattern: E+R+E+R = event
+ reaction + explanation + response.

55 John 9

That is the pattern on the day of Pentecost - the Spirit comes and people hear the message in their own language (event), and people think they are drunk (reaction). Peter gives an explanation that focuses on Jesus, and 3,000 people respond!

The same pattern can be seen when Peter and John heal the lame man (Acts 3) and when the gospel crosses cultures to the household of Cornelius - Cornelius and Peter each have dreams, and each reacts to his dream differently. Peter gives an explanation that focuses on God's story in Jesus and the household is swept into the kingdom on the wind of the Spirit. (Acts 10)

What kind of 'event' creates that first reaction today? It may be a healing or an answer to prayer which leaves people with a 'God-incident' that needs some explaining. It may be one of those acts of kindness that feels so out of place in a callous and calculating world. It may be the commitment of the local church to cancelling Third World debt or campaigning to save the local playground. Something catches people's attention and raises questions.

It is then that we must have the courage and the courtesy to set the event in the larger story of God's love shown to us in Jesus. Their response is not our responsibility. Our job is simply to tell the story. The Spirit will do the rest.

Of course the events that trigger the conversation may not be so positive. Bereavement or some crisis can lead to people asking deep questions - possibly aggressive questions about why it has happened, or more openly about what is going on.

The mystery of suffering is never explainable. Story is always the best answer - a story from our own experience or about someone we know -which speaks of how others have found God's help through tough times. The story is a sign that suffering is not an ultimate barrier to faith. For many it has been God's gateway to their hearts.

And then there are current events in the news. After the terrifying sight of the collapse of the Twin Towers in New York on 11 September 2001, many people felt that the world had shaken beneath their feet. One minister was stopped in the street by a very frightened woman who asked him to pray for her. That was the first time anyone had accosted him in that way.

It is a good thing to pray about the daily news. What do I think about what is going on? What is a Christian take on this? Where is God in the chaos? What would Jesus do here? When the conversation comes up at the coffee break or over the water cooler, we have as much right as anyone else to that opinion. Let's not pretend our view is the last word. Just throw it into the pot and see what happens. For somebody it might just be the fragment of truth that switches on the light.

I often find that some of the more angry psalms are helpful for being honest with God at times when the news is bad. On that 'day that changed the world', the American Bible Society had portions of the psalms on the streets of New York by the afternoon. There is no need to be embarrassed about our God at these times. It is the one time when people feel that their little story of the world no longer makes sense. Only a God who can bear the hammering of our anger against him can carry us through the chaos.

You see the pattern: event + reaction + explanation + response.

And for those who feel a little more courageous, why not take advantage of the phone-in programmes on the radio or TV to introduce a Christian viewpoint? The advice from the experts is to have your point written down clearly, to keep to the point and make it succinctly -and know when to stop. This is not a time to preach. It is simply a time to remind a secular public that the rumour of God is still rumbling around the country.

PETER

David, if I am really put on the spot about my faith, where do I begin?

DAVID

Let me point out a very important distinction: a witness tells his or her own personal story; an evangelist tells God's story.

What's the difference?

A witness - tells his/her own (human) story

An evangelist - tells God's story

How do I tell my story? - being a witness

Paul gives us a good example in the way he shares his own story as recorded in Acts 22. The crowd in Jerusalem wanted to murder Paul since some people had stirred up ill-feeling against him, so he was given permission by the Roman commander to tell his side of the story, and this is how he does it:

1. 22:1 - 5 Paul tells them what his life was like before he was a Christian
2. 22:6 - 13 Paul tries to explain how Jesus came into his life
3. 22:14 - 21 Paul shares what his life has been like since then, with its joys and trials.

If you do get a chance to share your own spiritual journey with someone, an easy way to do it is to set it out in three simple parts just as Paul did:

1. What I was like before I was a Christian

2. How God came into my life

3. What I'm like now and the difference it's made

Those of us who can't quite divide life into three parts like this might find the story of Peter a better template for our story. John Drane suggests that Peter's experience gives a different angle on telling our story:

1. *I believe in God* - Peter was a believer in God before he met Jesus.

2. *Jesus seems a good guy* - Peter answers the call to discipleship (Mark 1:14-20).

3. *I need to think this through* - Peter sees Jesus for who he really is, the Messiah and Son of God (Mark 8: 27-30).

4. *Can I really love him this much?* - Peter has to struggle with his emotions of fear and love in working out his loyalty to Christ. (John 18:15-27; 21:1-23)

5. *Who is God? Who am I? What is this all about?* -Peter has his whole worldview challenged by his encounter with Cornelius. (Acts 10:1-48)

6. *Sharing myself and my faith* - Peter travels, writes, suffers and eventually dies for Christ in Rome. (1 Peter).

Perhaps our story would read something like this:

I can't remember a time when I didn't believe in God. Through a Christian friend, I began to take Jesus more seriously. His life and approach to people marked him out as special. There was a stage when I began to see that he was more than that, and that he was asking me to follow him. That was a struggle - and it still is. I feel I let him down so often, but he never gives up on me.

The longer I live with Jesus, the bigger my world becomes. He seems to embrace all sorts. That's a real challenge. Following Jesus is tough at times, but, by the grace of God, I want to hang in there. I can't imagine life without him.

Over to You

Try writing out your story in the style of Paul.

Now try it in the style of Peter.

What have you discovered?

How do I tell Jesus' story? - being an evangelist

The good news is that God doesn't want us all up there telling the whole story! The New Testament talks about some having the gift of being an evangelist, but not all.

With our emphasis on the pastoral ministry, the Church of Scotland has been slow to encourage and support those who feel called to be evangelists, but recent General Assemblies have recognised the importance in affirming this calling. They have set aside certain individuals with very different styles of evangelism (multi-media, traditional proclamation, storytelling and so on).

There are opportunities now in Scotland to help train and encourage those with this gift of evangelism:

• **Christian colleges** offer modules on evangelism.

• **Mission Scotland** has received funding from the Billy Graham organisation to put in place an **Institute of Evangelists** [56].

• The **Herald's Trust** offer courses [57].

We have to confess that we have grossly under-resourced this calling when we consider Peter Wagner's suggestion that *perhaps as many as ten per cent of Christians have the gift of evangelism.*[58]

You may be in that ten per cent if you have a real passion for sharing the gospel, enjoy seeing people come to faith and feel more at home on the edge of the church than at the centre.

William Abraham in *The Logic of Evangelism* offers a refreshing view of what an evangelist might look like:

---

[56] Contact - Mission Scotland Offices
[57] Contact - The Herald's Trust
[58] C. Peter Wagner, Your Spiritual Gifts Can Help Your Church Grow, MARC, 1979, p 177

And to what shall we compare the church's evangelists? They need to be shepherds who know their sheep and can find them without driving them further from the fold. They need to be news announcers who get the message straight and make it known clearly to the nations without resorting to the sensationalism of Madison Avenue advertising techniques. They need to be lawyers who can argue their clients' cases with integrity, good humour and grit. They need to be midwives who can help nature and grace to bring children of God to birth through the pain of repentance and the joy of faith. They need to be physicians of the soul who can link the lost and weary with the healing medicine of the Kingdom. They need to be mothers who bring their little ones to be bathed in the waters of baptism...to be fed at the breasts of mother church.[59]

So by all means, let's encourage those who feel they have this calling. We don't need to fly in folk from other countries when we've got local talent who can help at local missions, talk at outreach events, or be part of a team that's trying to plant churches among new groups of people.

Everyday Evangelists

Some of the most effective evangelists I've come across didn't go to any theological college. They had earned their degrees in the 'university of life'; ordinary folk who spoke in a language people could understand.

---

59 Abraham, William, *The Logic of Evangelism*, Hodder and Stoughton, 1991, pp106-7

I'm thinking of people like Geordie Aitken. Originally from Bridgeton in Glasgow, he was living in East Kilbride when I was minister of the West Kirk. He died a few years ago and is sadly missed but his stories and expressions still make me laugh:

- 'If I join your church Davy, I don't want to be 'pew fodder'; I want to be used.'

- 'Jesus will accept anyone, because he took me, and I've got more hang-ups than a Chinese laundry.'

- 'Don't worry if you're having trouble getting accepted by that church, hen. Jesus has been trying to get in there for years.'

- 'The ground at the foot of the cross is level - there's no "high heid yins".'

After being heckled and harassed for ages by some clown in a meeting, Geordie pinned the guy by the throat to the wall: 'You want proof there's a God? The fact that you're still alive is proof! If I wisnae a Christian, I'd have taken yer heid right aff yer body, ya bampot!' Echoes of Geordie's 'old life' were still there - but no longer dictated his behaviour.

His heart was always for those who were on the streets and his vision and faith was instrumental in setting up the 'Loaves and Fishes' charity which still works in and around Glasgow today.

And I'm thinking of May Nicholson who has worked tirelessly in housing schemes in Paisley, Dundee and Glasgow with single parents and victims of abuse:

'Once the wee lassie had shared her problems with me, Davy, I asked her if she wanted to join me in a prayer and she gave her heart to the Lord.'.

Some people are just naturals!

Beyond Evangelists to Missionaries

Witnesses and evangelists obviously have their place when we're talking about sharing the good news. But in today's post-Christian society where many people can be two or three generations removed from any kind of organised church attendance ('I think my great-gran used to go to church'), some are recognising that the UK is now a mission field. We need to send out missionaries.

One prophetic voice is George Lings of the Sheffield Centre who researches the changing patterns of our culture and the shape of our gospel response:

Today, the more we step way beyond the fringe out to the non-churched, the less we can simply evangelise and think of bringing people back to a church which they have rejected and (which) is foreign to their culture.

The apostolic task is more demanding and more uncertain - to be sent out to journey with God and them, finding with them, not forcing on them, forms of an indigenous church that will continue to speak to their culture …

To be an evangelist is now only half the task. The skills of the cross-cultural missionary will be highly relevant. CMS (the Church Missionary Society) now has more mission partners in the UK than any other single country in the world.

… We must challenge those who only have the old evangelism paradigm in their heads.[60]

60 George Lings, *The Shape of Things to Come*, Paper for Joint Church Army Focus Group Conference, October 2002, p. 8

On his return to the United States, after working with the Masai tribe in East Africa, Vincent Donovan wrote:

I realised, when I came back to America, that on the home front I had left behind me one of the most exotic tribes of all - the young people of America. They have their own form of dress …food, music, ritual, language, values -these are the things that make up a tribe, or a subculture as they have been called. It is to that tribe, as they are, that the gospel must be brought…

You must have the courage to go with them to a place that neither you nor they have been before.61

The general call to all is to be witnesses. The special calling for some is to be evangelists. The overall calling is to mission - to be sent out to meet people where they are with the good news of Jesus Christ.

A Cross Cultural Experience

Peter was taken out of his comfort zone to speak to Cornelius.
Acts 10: 1-48

What experiences have you had of crossing into another culture?

What culture groups might God be calling you to connect with?.

.61 Vincent Donovan, preface to 2nd edition of *Christianity Rediscovered*

Peter - any final thoughts on passing on this good news?

Peter

Pass on the Story

When Peter had his chance to speak in the marketplace in Jerusalem and in the home of Cornelius in Caesarea, his message was virtually the same: he told the story of Jesus as a good man through whom God worked in remarkable ways; he told about Jesus' death and his resurrection and how that was, in line with God's story, etched into the lives of the Jewish people; he always added 'of this we are witnesses'.

At Jerusalem, he invited the people to turn from their sins, to trust in Christ for forgiveness and to receive the promised Holy Spirit. At Caesarea, the Holy Spirit beat him to it. Only God can make God real to people. We tell the story. God makes it a reality.

We are living through a time when people know almost nothing about the story of Jesus - or only the vaguest snippets. One of the best things we can do is to give people the chance to think about the whole story for themselves.

For people who still read, it is worth giving them a gospel to read through as a short story and then arrange to talk about it. For those who prefer the Internet, try www.rejesus.com for a selection of gospel stories, prayers and comments.

Some adventurous churches around Scotland tried making their own films recently. Around 40 churches were given a camera and a story from the Gospel of John. Over a period of weeks they were to produce a five minute presentation of that story located in their own community. At the end they had an 'Oscar Ceremony'. That kind of creative idea can involve people who are not at all sure about the gospel, but who enjoy the creativity and the technology to connect with the story in a new way - or for the first time.

If you are issuing gospels, here are a few thoughts. The shortest gospel is Mark. His abrupt ending ('They were afraid...') might have been Mark's way of inviting his readers to join in the story for themselves - no need to be a superhero!

Luke's Gospel is useful. That is the one with the Christmas story and the Good Samaritan and the Prodigal Son. If there are any stories floating around in the residual memory of our culture, these would be the most likely tags of familiarity. There are two other advantages to using Luke: it is available on a 90-minute video (called simply *Jesus*), and it has a sequel (the book of Acts).

Matthew's gospel has the Sermon on the Mount as a core section, though the genealogy at the beginning is a bit daunting. But, then again, I know a young man who came to faith through reading one of these genealogies, tracing Christ's roots in history and realising that God's Son was the way for him to become God's child too.

John's gospel was written for the specific purpose that people may 'believe Jesus is the Christ, the Son of God, and, that by believing you may have life in his name.' [62].

62 John 20:31

As a young man, that was the version of the story which gripped my imagination and called me to faith in Christ. For days, the mysterious and elusive character of Jesus seemed to speak to me from the words of John.

The Holy Spirit took that story and forged a connection with the story of my life which has held firm for almost forty years. Of this I am a witness.

9. The Way of Identity

*'I cannot forget a sculpture which I saw in
the open-air sculpture garden in Minneapolis.
It is called "Without Words" by Judith Shea.
There are three shapes.
One of them, the dominant one, is a bronze raincoat,
standing upright, but empty, with no one inside...
We are not destined to be empty raincoats.'*

Charles Handy [63]

63 Handy, Charles, *The Empty Raincoat,* Arrow Books,1995, p 1

PETER:

We live in a logo culture when *national* identity has weakened, and we are pre-occupied with our *personal* identity, 'Who am I?' What we have and what we wear marks us out as 'cool' or 'uncool'. The dark side of the consumer culture creates deep exclusive divides of who is 'in' and who is 'out'. Descartes' dictum was '*Cogito ergo sum*' -I think, therefore I am. Today's dictum might well be '*Tesco ergo sum*' - I shop, therefore I am.

The roots of personal identity are looser than they have ever been in our history. Globalisation of communication and massive migration create disconnections from local geographical roots. Serial family life, IVF fertility treatments and advances in genetics, all contribute to uncertainties about biological roots and personal identity. If belonging leads to believing in God, then lack of belonging leads to lack of believing in ourselves.

We know who we truly are when we become children of God by becoming brothers and sisters of Christ. That is the ultimate homecoming. 'Amatus, ergo sumus.' - I am loved, therefore we are.

Henri Nouwen writes for a friend who is a secular Jew, but would like to have the Christian message spelled out in terms that he can grasp. Nouwen sums up his message in one word 'Beloved'. He explains that he has picked this up from Jesus of Nazareth and, in particular from the account of Jesus' baptism:

> Fred, all I want to say to you is, 'You are beloved', and all I hope is that you can hear these words as spoken to you with all the tenderness that love can hold. My only desire is to make these words reverberate in every corner of your being, 'You are Beloved.' [64]

64 Nouwen, Henri JM, *Life of the Beloved: Spiritual Living in a Secular World*, Hodder and Stoughton, 1993, p 26

In all our communication of the gospel, that is the bottom line: that women and men whose lives are bruised and broken, discover that from the heart of the universe, they are 'Beloved' .

The issue of identity recurs throughout life: in childhood, in adolescence, in the life choices of our twenties, in midlife and as we face the opportunities and challenges of the Third Age. Each phase of life offers times for review of the foundations on which life has been built and to consider the basis for the next phase of life. The choices, changes and crises of birth, marriage, divorce, illness or death are times when we review life and faith. These are the places for coming alongside and creating the context for the awakening or reawakening of faith in Jesus Christ.

Life in the Afternoon'

We cannot live the afternoon of life according to the programme of life's morning, for what was great in the morning will be little at evening, and what in the morning was true, will at evening have become a lie.'
Carl Jung

What does that say to you about your life?

What does that say about others on their journey of faith?.

The Critical Journey

Robert Guelich and Janet Hagberg formed a team as theologian and psychologist to investigate spiritual journeys of different kinds. Their findings are contained in their book called *The Critical Journey* [65].

They describe the first stages of the journey as **discovery**, **belonging** and **working** as we engage in the spiritual search, throw in our lot with fellow searchers or fellow believers and then work together on the basis of that belief. Then comes a period of questioning when we wonder what it is all about.

At that point we hit 'The Wall' - a point of impasse where there seems to be no way over, round or through it. All that we have believed feels hollow and empty. It is a devastating experience which rings true for many Christians who face a crisis of faith perhaps in mid life. The good news is that there is life beyond 'The Wall'. Beyond the wall we learn to 'live with uncertainty' but with a deeper confidence in God.

These insights are important personally and pastorally, but they can also be significant evangelistically. This journey applies to faith of any kind - and everyone believes in something…even if it is a declared faith that there is no God. (That is a brave act of faith).

Many people are living by faith in their own ability, in money, in a significant relationship or whatever. Then life throws them a curved ball and they begin to question their basis of faith. These are moments of opportunity to help people move from a shaky basis of faith to faith in Christ.

---

[65] Hagberg, Janet O and Guelich, Robert A, *The Critical Journey - Stages in the Life of Faith*, Word Publishing, 1989

Jesus told the familiar story of the man who built his house on sand and the man who built on rock. When the flood and storm came, the house on the sand fell and the house on the rock stood firm. When the crises of life come, people discover where they have built their house.

If we may play with Jesus' image a little, the crises can sweep away the sand, but reveal the rock underneath. Our job is to help people rebuild on the rock.

Learning from Jesus
Read the account of the two builders.
Matthew 7:24-27
Think of examples of 'building on sand' today.
Where have you seen life's storms opening
people to rethinking and rebuilding?

One Foot in Eden

The gospel of God's grace, by which we discover we are 'beloved', applies to every stage of life. One person who has written about this is Philip Newell in his book, *One Foot in Eden - a Celtic view of the Stages of Life.*[66]

To change the style and pace a little, we offer some of his insights summarised as a basis of meditation. We invite you to consider the stage of life that is relevant to you or to a person whom you want to see discovering the love of God. Take the biblical phrase that is suggested and let it rest in your mind for a time, recognising the grace of God's promise embedded in the words. Then pray the 'breathing prayer' - breathing in and out with the thoughts suggested.

[66] Newell, Philip, *One Foot in Eden - a Celtic View of the Stages of Life*, SPCK 1998 .

There are people in our society today who are very familiar with this pattern of breathing meditation. You may find this approach to reflecting on the love of God helpful. Try it for yourself first and then pass it on to others.

You may find it helpful to use music during these meditations. Choose music without words which speaks to you of God's love and God's holding strength.

Meditation and Reflection

Birth   **the grace of life's sacredness**
The child born of you will be holy. (Luke 1:35)

Breathe in   Think of what God has planted in us or
                our children.

Breathe out   Think of God bringing what is holy out of us
                or our children.

Childhood   **the grace of wonder and trust**
To such as these belongs the kingdom of God.
(Luke 18:16)

Breathe in   Think of childhood times.
Breathe out   Look for signs of the kingdom in these moments.

Adolescence the 'uncomfortable grace' of awakenings
Why were you searching for me? (Luke 2: 49)

Breathe in   Remember the awakenings of adolescence.
Breathe out   At what points was God searching for you
                and you for God?

Early adulthood   **the 'risk-taking' grace of passion**
My house shall be called a house of prayer.
(Luke 19:46)

Breathe in   Feel the passion of Jesus' words.
Breathe out   Where does your passion lie?

Middle years   **the grace of commitment to love**
As I have loved you, love one another.
(John 15:12)

Breathe in   Focus on times when you have
known yourself loved by God.
Breathe out   Think of a person who needs your love
and commitment.

Old age   **the grace of wisdom and stillness**
And the Holy Spirit rested on him. (Luke 2:25)

Breathe in   Receive the truth of the Spirit resting on
you and those older than you.
Breathe out   Seek the wisdom of being centred
on God.

Death   **the grace of coming home**
Into your hands I commend my spirit. (Luke 23:46)
Breathe in   Recognise the hands of God holding
you and those who are dying .
Breathe out   Release life back into the hands of God.

Think now of a person who would find that approach helpful at
this stage in their journey. You might like to copy it out and pass
it to them.

David, you're a very practical guy. Would you like to show us how people know they are 'beloved' of God through human expressions of love? What you might call 'a conspiracy of kindness'?

David

The Conspiracy of Kindness
'Kindness is a language which the dumb can speak, the deaf can understand.'
(C.N. Bovee)[67]

My mum still reminisces about the days before she was married. She used to work for a clothing manufacturer in Stockwell Street in Glasgow in the late 1940's, just after the war. 'The only job we've got for you, Jessie, is for someone who's prepared to stand and iron all day!' 'Oh that's fine, I quite enjoy ironing!' I know, it seems crazy - she enjoyed it then and all the way through family life, she enjoyed it as long as she was fit enough and able to do it.

When my kids got older, they used to ask, 'What's in that big plastic bin-bag, Dad?' 'Oh it's just some ironing for your Gran. She likes to do your kiddies' clothes.' (I usually tried to sneak a few of my shirts in there as well.)

I saw an advert in the local paper recently: 'Ironing - so much per bag.' My mum could have been a millionaire! But money was the thing furthest from her mind - it was just a simple act of kindness. 'Mum, you're an Angel'.

---

[67] Quoted by Steve Sjogren, *Conspiracy of Kindness*, Vine Books, 1993, p. 9

And my Dad - he could just have painted our bedroom walls magnolia, but he took a few nights to put up the Pixie and Dixie wallpaper we wanted (all right - it was an older version of Tom and Jerry!). He made my brother and me the sturdiest sledges in the street. He constructed the fastest bogey (4-wheel cart).

People are kind. Anybody can be kind. And with stories like the Good Samaritan and acts like washing the feet of his disciples Jesus encourages his church to be kind. And anyone can be kind! If ten per cent of the people in any church are gifted in the special ministry of evangelism, then this is the job of the 90 per cent - acts of kindness, servant evangelism.

Steve Sjogren says he's often asked to explain servant evangelism in a nutshell. In his moving and powerful book he describes it as

> 'demonstrating the kindness of God by offering
> to do some act of humble service with no strings
> attached.' [68]

He gets his church involved in simple acts of kindness and often gets striking responses. His teams will try anything from windscreen washing and doing gardens to giving out free coffees or cold drinks and distributing light bulbs. (Well - you know we all run out of them!)

In case you don't get round to reading the book, let me share his "five discoveries that empower evangelism":

1. People listen when I treat them like friends.
2. When I serve, hearts are touched.
3. As I serve, I redefine the perception of a Christian.
4. Doing the message precedes telling the message.
5. Focus on planting not harvesting.[69]

---

68 Steve Sjogren, *Conspiracy of Kindness*, Vine Books, 1993, pp. 17 & 18
69 *Ibid* pp.101 - 126

Many people know that some of the large-scale city missions are beginning to use servant evangelism as part of their programme -sending teams in to clean up an area of the city on a day when an evening concert is scheduled for example.

I want to share a couple of small-scale local examples - because these are things that anyone could do!

A Story from the East

The first story is from the east of Scotland and was told to me by one of the members of the church involved.

> One Sunday, the flower committee had the great idea that "instead of just distributing the flowers to our own members as usual after the Sunday service, why don't we just give them out to a few folk in the village?" Brilliant, a good idea, so that's what they did.
>
> A few days later, one of the church members was in the building and there was a knock at the door. It was a man who asked: 'Is this the church that gave out the flowers a few days ago to people in the village?'
> 'Yes, why? Can I help you?'
> 'Have you got a kitchen?'
> 'Yes, why?'
> 'Would you mind if I had a look at it?'
> 'No, not at all; come away round.'
> He had a good look round.
> 'Right, I'll tell you what it is. My wife was one of the folk that got the flowers and no-one's ever done that for us before - she was really touched. Your kitchen's in a bit of a state, and what I do is, I fit kitchens. I'd like to fit you out with a new kitchen.'

A Story from the West

The second story is from the Glasgow area and it was the minister who shared this.

> The congregational board had been discussing how fortunate they were with the local school they had and how much they appreciated the teachers there and the way they cared for the kids. They wanted to express their thanks in some small way without embarrassing the staff too much.
>
> They discovered there was an evening staff meeting coming up, so they arranged to provide a good supply of trays of home-made sandwiches and baking. The teachers were thrilled with this simple act of kindness.
>
> The minister went on to suggest that it might be a good idea to do something similar for others - especially those who are often taken for granted in the service sectors of our communities.

'You're an angel'. And do you know what? Angels can have fun! They actually enjoyed it! The folk in Steve's book who were washing cars, and the folk in the local projects mentioned above really had fun doing their bit.

Evangelism then becomes a by-product of our fun. A newcomer to servant evangelism recently confided in me, 'You know, you can't pay to have this much fun in the world.' [70]

You don't need to be trained, you don't need to go to seminars, you don't need to wait till you're ready, you don't need to be perfect, you don't need to be afraid about making mistakes.

70 Steve Sjogren, *Conspiracy of Kindness*, Vine Books, 1993, p. 160 .

You need to go out and do it!
You're an angel.

David

Peter, I enjoyed that bit!
Back to you,
to sum up this section.

Peter

My Way is not Your Way

Every person is different. We see the world differently. We learn differently. We are motivated by different things. We pick up information in different ways. We relate to the world and to people in different ways. We relate to God in different ways.

Some people will 'hear' that they are beloved by the gentle words of a friend or the story we tell of God's love. Some will see God in action in that conspiracy of kindness. Others will enjoy a quiet space to meditate and open the door to God's Holy Spirit to speak at levels deeper than words or actions.

The popular Myers-Briggs Personality Indicator shows that some of us gain energy by being extrovert or introvert. Some of us pick up information through our senses and others by intuition. Some arrive at decisions by thinking things through while others are more 'feeling' people. Others again take life as it comes while others plan it out.

All this means that different people will find God in different ways. My way is not necessarily your way. God's way with me is not necessarily God's way with you. At the heart of all our faith sharing is respect for the other person - respect for his or her individual identity while praying that they find a deeper identity in knowing they are loved by God in Christ.

God knows each personality. As we read the gospels, we can see Jesus touching extrovert Peter and introvert John. He wins the thinking accountant Levi and Mary Magdalene, a woman of passion. Martha, the practical house-wife and Mary, her quiet meditative sister are both on board. Shy Andrew and questioning Thomas find their place in the story.

One person may come to faith through working for Christian Aid and coming to believe that God wants a better world. Another may need a space to be quiet or walk through a Labyrinth to let go before meeting God. Some will need to have all the proof of the resurrection spelt out to be sure they are not being conned. Some will come because God brought healing through prayer to them or someone close to them.

The story of Jesus intersects with the personal stories of individuals that are very different. The history of the Christian church over 2,000 years has seen people become followers of Jesus from every continent and culture. He is the cross-cultural Christ. People have come to faith in Christ as children and as old men on their death beds. He is the intergenerational Christ. People have followed him from every walk of life. He is the social-equality Christ.

Whatever the way or the means, the encounter with the living Christ is a mystery.

10. The Way of Mystery

*'When you meet another person, take off your shoes
for you are on holy ground.
God has been there before you.'*
Gerard Hughes [71].

---

[71] Unsourced quotation attributed to Gerard Hughes

Peter

It's a mystery. Anyone who has watched a person discover that Jesus Christ is alive is as amazed as the person making the discovery. It is one of the greatest privileges in the world. How a person meets this risen Christ and 'knows' the gift of forgiveness and new life - that is sheer mystery!

Only God can make God known. That is why prayer is at the heart of any concern for evangelism. Prayer recognizes that this is God's business and we are invited into a junior partnership. Prayer is living in communion with God, learning to notice the divine presence in the everyday. Sometimes that is focused and intentional. Sometimes it is 'on the hoof' and spontaneous.

A popular hymn affirms that 'I will hold your people in my heart.'[72] That is a powerful image for any person who wants to share the gospel with another person. We speak to God about people before we speak to people about God.

In the Old Testament, the High Priest entered the presence of God on behalf of the people of Israel. One symbol of that role was the breastplate he wore, studded with twelve gems, each representing a tribe of Israel. Thus, when the High Priest entered the presence of God, he carried the people of Israel with him.

I wonder if he stood in that Holy of Holies and said to God: 'Here I am with Judah, and Reuben and Dan and … right through to the little tribe of Benjamin.'

Certainly the writer to the Hebrews imagines Jesus, the great High Priest coming into the presence of God saying: 'Here am I and the children whom God has given me' (Hebrews 2:13).

---

72 *Common Ground*, St Andrew Press,1998, Song No 50

Imagine yourself coming into the presence of God, being introduced to the Father by Christ our elder brother, with these words. Now imagine yourself before the Father, naming the people you want to see embraced in his love and imagine their names written on your chest -each one a gem in the sight of God:

'Here I am with Tom and Kirsty and Margaret and...'

Recognise the Father's love for them. Come, Holy Spirit, and make that love known to them in ways they can understand.

Miracle and Mystery

C.S. Lewis, in his autobiography, *Surprised by Joy*, tells of struggling for months with the gospel. Somehow he couldn't get past the 'unrea-sonableness' of the message. His story seems to me not too different from that of another famous British intellect, Bertrand Russell.

Both of these men asked the same questions and came up with the same unsatisfactory answers early in life. Both describe a tremendous struggle with the gospel, of how they got into the issues of the gospel, dissected them point by point, but still could not come to belief. Though they asked many of the same questions, their conclusions were very different.

Russell wrote of his struggle and conclusion that God is not real in his book *Why I am not a Christian*. Lewis' story took a significant turn one day, almost to his surprise. The arena for battle shifted from Lewis' head to his heart. As he tells it, he was on the back of his brother's motorcycle on his way to the zoo.

He says, 'All that I know is that when I got on that motorcycle I did not believe in Jesus and that by the time we arrived at the zoo I was a believer.' [73] **When we rightly understand evangelism, we recognise that it is both a miracle and a mystery how any of us come to know Christ.**[74]

That was at the heart of Jesus' conversation with Nicodemus.[75] The work of the Spirit is as mysterious as the wind in the trees. We do not know where it comes from or where it goes. But as the Spirit passes through, lives are changed - like a new birth from God above. Only God's Spirit can create life fit for the kingdom of God.

The Shy Search

The wind of the Spirit is blowing in our culture today creating a hunger for God. Many people are searching for spiritual reality. The word 'spirituality' appears in the language of health care and business management. Spirituality fills the bookshops with themes from healing to angels, Reiki to Tarot, horoscopes to ley lines. People are searching for a sense of connectedness to the world. We must meet people as fellow travellers on their journeys of faith.

73 Lewis CS,*Surprised by Joy*, New York: Inspirational, 1987, p130
74 Steve Sjogren, *Conspiracy of Kindness*, Vine Books, 1993, pp. 124 & 125
75 John 3:1-21.

Rob Frost, a Methodist evangelist of 30 years' experience, has recently published the book, *A Closer Look at New Age Spirituality*. He opens with these words:

> For too long the church has seen the New Age
> movement as a threat, an enemy, and a source
> of evil in the world. I began to write this book as a
> diatribe of Bible verses and theology condemning it.
> I repent.
> Since meeting some of those involved in New
> Age activity, hanging around their bookstalls and
> fairs and hearing them talk of their genuine quest
> for reality, I've changed my perspective. Now, I'm
> asking: what can I learn from the emerging New Age
> spirituality? What can it teach me? How can it help
> me?[76]

Fellow Travellers on the Journey
The work of David Hay and Kate Hunt on the spirituality of people who do not go to church has also challenged many of us to take a new look at the spiritual journeys of the contemporary seeker and to walk humbly alongside the mystery of that quest.

76 Frost, Rob, *A Closer Look at New Age Spirituality*, Kingsway, 2001, p 9

The Spirituality of People who don't go to Church[77]

Some key findings:
People are 60% more likely to speak of a spiritual experience today than 15 years ago.
People are 50% more likely to speak of answered prayer.
People are confused by church and want a 'church for beginners'.
In every culture there are 'valves' that open people to spiritual experiences.
The church used to do that for people, but now it is a valve that 'closes' people off.

What does that suggest about our approach to sharing our faith?
Where are the 'valves' that open people up to spiritual reality today?

 For the Christian, spirituality has a focus. It is about living the whole of life in the presence of God as we know him in Jesus Christ. Sharing faith in this context is not about arguing our case more cogently. It is about living the life more consistently. We need to be 'interpreters of the inner landscape' for fellow explorers.

Our role model is Jesus meeting the confused couple on the Emmaus Road, listening, interpreting and eventually revealing himself. No techniques. No gimmicks. No sound-bites. No clever strap-lines. Just people living close to God in a way that helps others come close to God.

[77] David Hay & Kate Hunt, *Understanding the Spirituality of People Who Don't Go to Church*, University of Nottingham, 2000..

The challenge is not to master the arguments of old style apologetics. The challenge is to become beginners again in the ancient art of prayer and reflective living:

> Where have we encountered God today?

> Was it a good moment or a tough time?

> Was it personal and internal?

> Was it an event or a happening around you?

> Was it in a time of focused prayer at the beginning of the day?

> As we reflect on the day, do we notice the smudge of God's fingerprints?

People discover God among people who are discovering God. If we are learning to discover God in the everyday, then others will tag along and find him too. The prophet Zechariah paints a lovely picture of the Jews going to worship God, and ten others join the queue:

> In those days, ten men from all languages will take firm hold of one Jew by the hem of his robe and say, 'Let us go with you, because we have heard that God is with you.' [78]

People are certainly on the look out for those who are living out an authentic spirituality. Draw on the mystery of God's wisdom and others will want to drink from the wells we dig.

---

[78] Zechariah 8:23

Learning from Jesus

Read about Jesus listening to the questions of the couple on the Emmaus Road.
Luke 24:13-35

How does Jesus offer a role-model for the listening evangelist?

Sharing Water from the Well

Imagine an early morning rendezvous with God. That may mean a candle and some quiet music. It may mean reading a psalm or a story from the gospels. You pray that psalm as though it was written for you -or for someone else facing the same situation as the psalmist.

The gospel story is about the stilling of the storm. You feel the wind and the sea. You hear the disciples and watch the action. You are in the presence of Jesus. You enter into conversation with him about what is happening. His words seem to come back to you in a very personal way.

You take your notebook and record a thought or insight for the day. You might write a short prayer for others. The ripples of prayer go out to family and friends, the local community or that headline in the news bulletin. The time ends and you walk into the day.

Later in the day, a friend is talking over a coffee about a big row that has blown up at work. You sense a connection with what you read or thought about in the morning. It helped you. It may help her. Tentatively you mention that you had been thinking about how God can bring.peace in the chaotic times. Does she think that God might still the storm at work? You promise to pray for her as she goes back to the office. The conversation moves on to other things.

There has been no rehearsing of special words. There has simply been an honest sharing of what you have been discovering about God. You share water from the well. No fuss. Then walk away. The rest is up to God. It's a mystery.

David, tell us some of the ways in which people are being helped to find God through this route of spiritual exploration.

David

Experience God rather than Explain about God

Peter, you are right. Many people today in our post modern society would have no reservations in sharing with you that they're on a spiritual search of one kind or another. But they are no longer interested in the 'Is it true?' questions. They want to know, 'Does it really work?'

People nowadays don't want to be told that they have to believe something because it's true for a number of reasons. What people really want today is to experience that truth for themselves.

Here are two approaches which enable people to pursue their spiritual search.

Essence

Rob Frost, the well-known Methodist minister, evangelist and broadcaster, is attempting to offer creative and imaginative ways into Christian spirituality through a new course called *Essence*. After exploring the issues surrounding mission in a New Age context, Rob put together what is described on the front cover as 'A six-session interactive programme to stimulate a deeper spiritual life, drawing from the teachings of Jesus and the Christian mystics.'

Alpha and other process evangelism courses most certainly have their place, but *"Essence* aims to start where a growing number of non-Christians are, with the issues that concern them, valuing their own spiritual experiences. The learning style is very experiential and involves things like relaxation exercises on the floor, making bracelets, smashing pots and modeling in dough. The Bible is used as a resource in all six sessions, each of which ends with a prayer in the name of Jesus." [79] The CD provided with the course contains helpful background music, songs, stories and meditations.

This is a genuine attempt to start where many enquirers are - caught up in the turmoil of modern life. It acknowledges that while they may have had a wide variety of spiritual experiences, they remain skeptical of institutional religion. This approach aims to enable them to consider the way of Jesus.

Rob pulled together a variety of people as he developed this course and I was privileged to be involved in part of the consultative process as the six sessions eventually took their final shape:

79 Mike Booker and Mark Ireland, *Evangelism - which way now?*, Church House Publishing, 2003, p. 177

1. The Journey So Far	- our own journey
2. The Journey Within	- who am I?
3. The Journey to a Better World	- the environment
4. The Journey to Wholeness	- pain and healing
5. The Journey to Spirituality	- prayer
6. The Journey to the Future	- hopes and dreams, life after death

The best place to run the course is a community centre or a club, or a large living room. Try it with a few other helpers, and then move people on to something else like *Alpha* or *Emmaus.*

The Labyrinth

Punch the word **Labyrinth** into your computer and you'll find plenty of information on numerous websites on this particular topic. I'm not going to say too much here, except that this is another real opportunity of engaging with all sorts of people beyond the normal reach of the church.

As can be seen from the diagram, the Labyrinth is set out as a 'journey towards God' with various 'reflection points' along the way. Some churches set up a temporary labyrinth in a church hall once a month, using pebbles and tea-lights to mark the route, with ambient music playing in the background. Some larger churches and cathedrals have space at the back of the sanctuary to keep a labyrinth permanently in position and are visited by students or workers on their lunch-break.

At the reflection points, people can be invited to:

• stop for a moment amidst all the hustle and bustle

• pick up a stone symbolising their burdens

• pray

• release their burden (drop stone into a bucket)

• think about their family

• say thank you

Advertise it in your area. Leave a few appropriate leaflets out on display. Train folk from the church café to be prepared to talk to anyone wanting to chat, and be prepared to witness miracles.

If your church is only half as full as it used to be, take out the pews at the back, create a café/gathering space with a welcoming, open environment and lay out a labyrinth.

People are still looking for sacred space - but it needs to be outsider-friendly and easily accessible

Who is the evangelist?

Lesslie Newbigin was a remarkable missionary in India from the 1950's to the 1970's. He tells the story of a village of 25 people who wanted to be baptised, and who therefore contacted him as the bishop. He had never heard of the village. He knew of no evangelistic work in the area. He visited them to hear their story.

Act I: An engineer had gone to the village to drill wells for water. He was a Christian who won the villagers' respect and admiration. He did not say much about his faith, but enough for them to know he was a follower of Jesus.

Act II: A Christian bookseller passed through the village selling gospels. The villagers bought one and read the stories communally in the village. They were fascinated by the person of Jesus.

Act III: A fiery Indian evangelist came through and spoke of how Jesus had died to forgive them and had been raised to offer them eternal life. They began to think that this part of the story was more important than they had realised.

Act IV: They sent to a neighbouring village where they knew there were some Christians. One of them was a farm labourer, who had broken his leg and could not work in the fields. He was carried to the first village where he stayed for a few weeks teaching them about Jesus.

Act V: They decided they wanted to become Christians and sent for Bishop Newbigin to baptise them.

Lesslie Newbigin asks, 'Who was the evangelist in that story?' Answer: 'The Holy Spirit'.

The Holy Spirit is the evangelist. We are partners in the mystery.

11. The Way of the Workaday Life

So here's what I want you to do, God helping you:
Take your everyday, ordinary life
your sleeping, eating, going-to-work, walking-around life -
and place it before God as an offering.
Embracing what God does for you
is the best thing you can do for him.'
Romans 12
The Message.

David

Many Christians live schizophrenic lives. There is little connection between Sunday worship and Monday work, but one of the major mission movements today is to heal that divided life. Increasingly, Christian people are recognising that they are sharing in God's mission as they go about their daily work.

Mark Greene, Executive Director of the London Institute for Contemporary Christianity, went right to the core of this issue when he shared this story about a primary school teacher:

> Becoming increasingly frustrated during normal Sunday church services by the lack of reference to the real lives people were having to cope with at home and at work, she eventually approached her minister with some hesitation and said:
>> 'Thank you for the prayers you offer regularly for the work I do as a Sunday School teacher for one hour every week. But do you know, no-one has ever prayed for me for the work I do as a primary school teacher for forty hours every week?!' [80]

It's a telling story isn't it? 'You're an angel' - but not just because you're involved with church work in our wee sub-culture once a week. 'You're an angel' - even (and especially) when you're coping with all the pressures and stresses of work and family life.

Mark goes into this whole area in much more detail in his book Thank God it's Monday - Ministry in the Workplace [81], and it's certainly worth looking at this and other resources (especially his article on being a 'full-time Christian worker' on the LICC website, www.licc.org.uk/ftcw) but I simply want at this stage, for the sake of our particular concerns, to refer to a couple of significant points he makes elsewhere.

80 Mark Greene - in the course of a presentation at "Mission Scotland", Stirling University, 2003
81 Mark Greene, Scripture Union, 2001

First, he points out that:

> The sacred-secular divide which keeps our day-to-day lives separate from our church lives has led to flawed theologies of church and outreach[82]

It's no wonder some people think church is irrelevant if we keep our lives 'packaged' into separate compartments where one important area of life has virtually nothing to do with another!

Secondly, he hints at the exciting possibilities if ordinary people just realised their potential for being workers for God, agents of change, bringers of peace. We've been saying the right kind of thing for a while, but we are still not good at resourcing ordinary people 'on the ground':

> Back in 1945, the Church of England published a book called Towards the Conversion of England. The section on evangelism came to this conclusion: 'We are convinced that England will never be converted until the laity use the opportunities for evangelism daily afforded by their various occupations, crafts and professions.'

82 'Imagine - How we can reach the UK', article for 'idea', Evangelical Alliance magazine, March/April 2003, p. 21
83 "Imagine - How we can reach the UK", article for "idea", Evangelical Alliance magazine, March/April 2003, p. 24.

David

Peter, you have had some experience working in the business sector in Edinburgh. Tell us more about that.

Peter

'You're an Angel.'

Christians reflect the image of God as creator as we choose to partner God in making and managing the world. We may share in God's redeeming process by making the world a better place for people, by fixing problems and healing life's hurts. We are representing God by the way we do our work, by the way we treat people, by our honesty and our dependability

In some of our cities, churches offer lunches and times for worship. Some have developed a strong Christian presence in the business community including courses to explore the Christian faith as a spiritual dimension to life. This helps to overcome the sense of 'double isolation' that people feel as work is divorced from worship and worship from work.

TTT

One church has a TTT spot every Sunday morning.
A person is invited to answer the question:
'Where will you be - This Time Tomorrow?'

The answer may range from office to classroom, from
caring for a dependent relative to commuting around the
world.
The congregation then prays for that person and
other people in similar situations.
This develops an '11 o'clock theology' -
where the members of the church are helping
each other at 11 o'clock on a Monday!

How might TTT be introduced in your church?

As people become increasingly isolated from the supportive services of the local church, they look to caring Christians for a listening ear in times of illness or bereavement. The prayerful interest of a colleague may be the first awareness of a God who cares. Those who are involved in workplace ministry find that they are drawn into the everyday issues that affect us all. People are more open to God than we imagine.

Learning from Jesus

Think of places where Jesus met people and some of the stories he told.
How many workplaces did he visit?
How many of his stories draw on workplace and business illustrations?
Imagine Jesus walking around your workplace.
He spots a piece of equipment or an everyday activity and begins:
'The kingdom of God is just like......'
Finish the sentence.
How can we learn from Jesus to help people see hints of God's presence in and around us?

Slaves of Time

A journalist is rushing through Rome's busy Fiumicino Airport. He is a foreign correspondent, desperate to catch his plane for London. He dashes through the departure lounge, talking all the time to his editor on his mobile phone.

He hits the queue and has to stand. He thinks about phone calls, e-mails, articles he must write. He skims his newspaper. An article catches his eye: *The One Minute Bedtime Story.* Here are fairy tales available in sixty-second sound-bites. He thinks of his two-year-old son who always wants another story, and for a moment, he considers buying a full set of these time-saving narratives.

Then he stops, horrified at himself. What is he dreaming about? He has become infected with the time-sickness that drives the world and destroys relationships. Does he have no more than a minute or two for his son?

The journalist closes his paper and begins to plan a book. It is called In Praise of Slow - How a World-Wide Movement is challenging the Cult of Speed. It is essential reading for those of us who have let the clock, the computer and the car become our masters rather than our servants.[84]

Many of our businesses are run by workaholics and supported by their victims; and the Holy Grail is the achieving of a work-life balance. What does the Christian church have to offer in this task-driven culture? Here is one church's response to that challenge:

Oasis

Oasis is the business ministry of St Cuthbert's and the other West End churches in the centre of Edinburgh. As the name suggests, it was set up to offer an oasis of peace from the pressurised business world of the fourth largest financial sector in Europe. In many ways it aims to offer the 'service of stillness' to an adrenalin-addicted culture.

[84] Honore, Carl, *In Praise of Slow*, Orion Books, 2004

Regular visits by the *Oasis* consultant and the associate minister to over 80 offices are shaped by three key questions:

1. How is the business doing?
2. What are the 'people' issues here?
3. If you were doing my job, how would you do it?

Answers to the first two questions suggest possible themes and ideas for discussion and events that will be helpful for people. Answers to the third question suggest endlessly creative ways of approaching our mission!

Lunchtime talks are held (at the invitation of businesses) in the larger offices on topics that meet the corporate or personal agenda: coping with change, stress, mediation, coaching, how to help a client or colleague who is bereaved or terminally ill. Speakers may or may not be Christians, but the events are hosted openly in the name of the churches. The talks are followed up by conversations with individuals over a coffee or a lunch at a later date.

These events must observe the parameters of courtesy within the premises of our host for the day. Any overt evangelism is inappropriate.

For those who want to think more about the spiritual dimension to life, *Oasis* has run five *Business Alpha* Courses in a local hotel. These are organised within the hour of an office lunch break, with 15 minute talks tailored to the business world. Over 200 people have attended these courses and a significant number have discovered 'an awakening or reawakening of faith in Jesus Christ.' They share in lunchtime discussions to secure and earth their faith in the everyday world of work.

The Horse-whisperer

*You may have seen the film or read the book
by Nicholas Evans.*

*A thoroughbred horse is injured in a traffic accident.
The vet can only do so much to help.
The owners call in the horse-whisperer who has learned the
ways of the native Americans.
He knows the horse's language.
He stays close to the horse and wins its trust.
The time comes when the horse has to be helped to face its
fear, and the horse-whisperer is the only one who can help it
because of the trust which has been established.
Together they make the break-through.*

*What does that story say to us about
'horse-whisperer evangelism'?*

First Wednesday, another *Oasis* initiative, offers a chance to open up a topic of concern in business life today. Mark Greene's video series on *Faith & Work* proved an excellent discussion starter.

Prayer networks support Christians in their work. Links between wealth-creating companies and a charity for re-housing homeless people fosters a sense of corporate social responsibility. A pastoral presence in the offices offers a listening ear to all who need it.

This partnership between the business community and the church has been nurtured over a period of 12 years and is now seen by the business community as a valued service to the offices and hotels in the area. Out of a working population of 10,000, we are still only scratching the surface - but at least we are scratching where people itch!

Being Church-Beyond-the-Congregation
Even if we do not have a business sector on our doorstep, it remains true that the people in our congregations are working in places where they need support to live their Christian faith with integrity.

Instead of creating artificial mission programmes, we should be pleasantly surprised to realise the mission that we already have through the people of God in their workplace. That is where people meet others of all generations and cultures. 'Every contact leaves a trace' is the first law of forensics.

Instead of training people to **'do church'**, let's train and release people to **'be church'** where they are, through friendship and mentoring. That way, we help people to live the gospel as 'whole life' disciples - the church-beyond-the-congregation.

What do I have to leave at the church door?

If I come to worship on Sunday as a person who has spent Monday to Friday in an office or shop, teaching children or fixing computers, driving a bus or doing brain surgery...what do I have to leave at the door?

How does Sunday worship relate to my working life on Monday morning?

Websites: www.oasisedinburgh.com and www.businessalphaedinburgh.com

12. The Way of Creativity

'I never think of my audiences as customers.
I think of them as partners.'

Actor Jimmy Stewart

Well, Peter! Should we be taking off the clerical robes and 'dog collar'? A lot of our evangelism has been done through preaching in churches, but what about other creative ways in which God speaks to people?

Peter

It's true, David, that many people find God through the arts. Music, film, photography, books, drama, video - all these media give people the chance to experience the good news. Often in the past, people have been spectators at special Christian events and 'seeker services', but today they are more likely to be participants.

People with expertise in computers and video for example, may be invited into a project to communicate the Easter story, and then, by being involved, discover its truth for themselves. Others, perhaps through joining the praise band or making music for a special occasion, may find the songs begin to mean something to them personally.

Christian clowns, jugglers and storytellers give people fresh insights into old truths - members of the audience may be ambushed by a parable.

In less formal ways, reflective worship can offer people the occasion to work with stones, paint, paper, water, pictures or drama - and the insights gained may connect with gospel truths. Hands-on experience can give God access to people's hearts.

The Open Mike

He goes to the pub four times a week.
He joins in the 'open mike' sessions when anyone can sing a
song, read a poem or tell a story.
He weaves the message of God into his
songs and stories and people sing and cheer.

When people step up to the open mike and forget their
words, others come up and play their guitar or drums to
help them along.
No-one puts them down.
When the struggler makes it to the end, everyone cheers - a
community of encouragement.
He sees signs of what the
New Testament church must have been like.
Check out the
church service at Corinth
(1 Corinthians 14:26-28)

Some of the pub-goers have tried church, but they have
not found this kind of open community where they can try
out their gifts. They are looking for a community where they
can contribute.

People learn in different ways. The assumption of much
evangelism has been that we simply 'hear the word'; and there
is a profound truth about having the 'ears to hear'. But Jesus
opened ears through stories and questions, through healings
and actions. He took his disciples into situations where they
experienced new things. They shared in the journey with him.
They saw and heard and touched the word of life.

Before 1970, most of our education was about 'listen and learn'. Since the 1970's, education has been about discovery and resourced-based learning. People 'hear' the good news as we offer multi-sensory approaches for them to discover the truth for themselves.

There are many creative ways of setting the context for the awakening or re-awakening of faith in Jesus Christ. Be imaginative. Jesus was.

And remember… being creative is not about being contrived. It may simply mean being a lively conversationalist who can help people make the connections with Christ that he is waiting to make clear.

Learning from Jesus

Read the story of the Samaritan woman at the well.
John 4:1-16

Sit in on this masterclass on being a Christian conversationalist.
Track the conversation and see how Jesus discloses himself to this woman.

What lessons will you take away?

Is that fair enough, David? People experience God in different ways, and the stories that are told through paintings, films, books and T.V. are all part of that.

David

Oh definitely, Peter. I'll never forget some of my earliest experiences of going to the pictures and I've been a movie fan ever since. It was a real treat when my parents took my brother and me to the cinema - and in those days you got to see two films, and you could queue up in front of a girl with a torch and pick an orange drink or an ice cream from her tray!

Then our school started a film club and showed *Great Expectations* – with that atmospheric opening scene on the mist-covered moors. I jumped out of my seat when the convict (Albert Finney) appeared out of the gloom and grabbed Pip!

Many will remember *The Gospel According to Peanuts* by Robert Short – a book which looked at the way the gospel was being communicated through Charles Schulz' *Peanuts* cartoons. Short, who is a pioneer in the study of religion and popular culture, has this to say:

The arts get under our skin far more effectively than direct discourse, far more effectively than a sermon[85]

When I'm in ordinary conversation with people, they talk about all sorts of things and I'm increasingly finding that God is never very far away.

85 Robert Short being quoted by Mark I. Pinsky, *The Gospel According to the Simpsons*, Westminster John Knox Press, 2001, p.180

There are threads of love, loss, suffering, grace, forgiveness, betrayal, envy, greed, lust and salvation woven through every book and film because this is the stuff of life - the stuff of day-to-day conversation.

Where is God? God is everywhere! And I want first of all to look at some contemporary music and film which is rich with the imagery of life in all its challenges, temptations, joys and suffering; and then I'll look at some of the ways in which churches are using different media.

Books

I've never been a fast reader. (My wife can get through about six books on holiday and I've got to allocate myself 20 pages a day to be sure to finish one!) But I really do enjoy it and get so much from almost any kind of book. Now I'm not going to list many books or authors here, but I'll mention a few by way of illustration. Why? Because most writers deal with real-life issues, whether we agree with the outcomes or not; and because some of these books might just be the ones my friends are reading and I want to be able to join in the discussions.

By all means go back to the classics (Shakespeare, Dickens, etc.); and there are so many good contemporary novels around, with more coming out every year. No sooner have I finished *Man and Boy* by Tony Parsons, than someone recommends *The Life of Pi* by Yann Martel. I just get through Phillip Pullman's *Northern Lights* when someone tells me there's a trilogy - *His Dark Materials*!

One of the most astute observers of life today has to be Nick Hornby, and his novel *How to Be Good* (Health Warning - don't read it if you can't cope with swearing) is packed full of witty comment on society, church, spirituality and family life.

A book like *Chocolat* (Joanne Harris) makes us think about the decline of traditional religion (the old church on one side of the street) and the rise of modern day secularism and consumerism (the temptation of the seductive new chocolate shop on the other side of the street).

Learning from Jesus

Jesus only wrote once as far as we know.
John 8:1-11

What do you think he wrote?
Does the fact that he never wrote (at least nothing on a material which has lasted) say anything to us?

Music

A lot of kids want to be rock stars when they grow up - even those who can't sing. Rock music is a medium which universally lends itself to expressing our deepest longings, loves and yearnings. It's amazing how many people I speak to, who don't perhaps count themselves as religious, but who are moved by all types of music - classical, rock, opera, choral, jazz, blues, pop and even rap.

I think it was Bono, the lead singer of U2, being interviewed in a T.V. documentary who said: There only are two kinds of music - gospel: running towards God; and blues: running away from God.

Many modern lyrics are of course fairly shallow and sometimes even vulgar and meaningless, but many songs contain moving and heart-searching observation and commentary:

'All the lonely people, where do they all come from?'
(The Beatles, Eleanor Rigby)

'That's me in the corner, losing my religion'
(R.E.M.)

'Imagine there's no heaven, it's easy if you try. No hell below us, above us only sky.'
(John Lennon, Imagine)

'And I'd join the movement, if there was one I could believe in. Yeah, I'd break bread and wine, if there was a church I could receive in.'
(U2, Achtung Baby, from Acrobat.)

'Well, I never pray. But tonight I'm on my knees, yeah. I need to hear some sounds that recognize the pain in me, yeah.'
(The Verve, Bittersweet Symphony.)

'Am I part of the cure, or am I part of the disease?'
(Coldplay, Clocks; from A Rush of Blood to the Head.)

The themes touched on by all these extracts are universal - these songs express feelings that we all experience at one time or another.

TV

I enjoy watching television. I'm not a great 'soaps' fan, but I do like *A Question of Sport*, *The Simpsons* and *Friends*. Some people say we're living now in the *Friends* generation. Many young people, having moved away from the parental home, but not feeling ready for marriage, are living in small communities of flat mates. And my kids certainly think it's hilarious the way the six characters vie for affection and affirmation, defend their own idiosyncratic personality traits, sometimes selfishly ignoring the needs of the others, sometimes touchingly compromising their own position so that the others might have a share of the limelight. It's all there - all the highs and lows of life.

The Simpsons

Years ago when I first saw the face of Bart Simpson on a wee boy's T-shirt, I thought it looked weird. Then I started to watch the cartoon itself and almost instantly warmed to the sheer genius of its production, the humour of its characters and the moving portrayal of life's little dramas:

Homer — the lazy overweight dad who takes most things for granted until he's drawn up short in one way or another

Marge — the patient, long-suffering mum with the impossible blue beehive hair-do

Bart — the son with 'trouble' written all over his face

Lisa — the talented daughter with the philosophical approach to things

Maggie — the baby sister

Tony Campolo says in the foreword to *The Gospel According to the Simpsons:*

> As an evangelical Christian, I find that The Simpsons provides me with a mirror that reflects my own religious life. ... Contrary to what some critics say, the Simpsons are basically a decent American family with good values. They go to church on Sunday. Homer and company triumphantly conquer the serious temptations of life, like adultery, and they even conquer some of the lesser sins, such as taking advantage of an illegal cable television hookup. Both the hypocrisies and the virtues of the Simpson family and the other characters on the show are too often my own.[86]

Marge Simpson is an angel:

She lives in the real world, she lives with crises, with flawed people. She forgives and she makes her own mistakes. She's a forgiving, loving person. She is absolutely saintly.[87]

Learning from Jesus

Jesus was the master story-teller.
Matthew 13:1-3

Which of Jesus' stories stands out in your memory?
Why is it special for you?

---

[86] Mark I. Pinsky, *The Gospel According to the Simpsons*, Westminster John Knox Press, 2001, pp. ix & x
[87] Kenneth Briggs - quoted by Mark I. Pinsky, *The Gospel According to the Simpsons,* Westminster John Knox Press, 2001, p. 108

Film

The interaction of religious faith and popular culture has been a growth area from the start of the 1990's. Although many of us had been touched by the messages of grace and forgiveness contained in some earlier films, there seems more recently to have been an enormous number of mainstream movies from *The Matrix* to *The Lord of the Rings* which have explored theological issues such as hope, good and evil, and transcendence.

There is now a growing body of academic work both in film studies and in theology addressing these areas, and many in the ministry of the Christian churches have seen opportunities and challenges in the dialogue between faith and film.

Jolyon Mitchell, based at Edinburgh University and author of *Visually Speaking*, addresses these issues; and the Centre for Christian Communication at St John's College, Durham has been exploring this dialogue for a number of years.

J. John and Mark Stibbe share some of their ideas about using films in their helpful books - *the Big Picture* and *the Big Picture 2*. Having used a variety of film clips in a series of alternative evening services, here's how they see the connections between the life of faith and film story lives:

> Using movies is a great way of connecting with contemporary culture. Movies are like visual parables and they make great illustrations of the timeless truths of the gospel...

> What did we learn? ... The first thing is that using movies helped Christians to bring God into their leisure time. In fact, it helped Christians to realise that we can hear God anywhere anytime.

Secondly, using the movies in teaching is a great way of communicating the truths of the Bible to a generation who know little about Christianity. This approach appeals to a post-modern generation where the primary organ of receptivity is the eye rather than the ear.

Thirdly ...movies and music, along with other forms of the creative arts, have a way of communicating truth at an affective rather than a purely cognitive level.

Fourthly, we kept the focus on Jesus Christ rather than a movie star by prioritising worship (during the services).

Movies are therefore a great way of getting people to think about life's ultimate questions. ... We are committed to the view that God speaks to people through films.[88]

In *The Big Picture,* they look at *Lara Croft, the Godfather (Parts I, II and III), Fargo, Titanic, The Matrix, Castaway, Saving Private Ryan,* and *Billy Ellio*t.

In *The Big Picture 2,* they examine this list of films under the following topics:
The Lord of the Rings: The Fellowship of the Ring - Overcoming the Darkness, *Simon Birch* - Fulfilling Your Potential, *The Green Mile* -There Can Be Miracles, *Bridget Jones's Diary* - Searching For Love,
What Women Want - The Art of Listening, *Unfaithful* - Choices and Consequences, *Minority Report* - Is My Future Fixed? And *Shrek* - It's What You Are on the Inside.

88 J. John and Mark Stibbe, *The Big Picture 2, Authenmtic Lifestyle, 2003, pp 3 & 4*

Scripture Union, Damaris Publishing and Christian Publicity Organisation have also taken the initiative and produced the excellent *Connect Bible Studies* (website - www.connectbiblestu dies.com). These studies look at contemporary issues in books, television and films, including: *Friends, James Bond 007, Billy Elliot, AI: Artificial Intelligence* and *His Dark Materials,* the Pullman trilogy.

As you can see, there's never going to be a shortage of material out there. So, what next?

How Can We Use All This?

Well, really, it's over to you, folks - the only limiting factor is your imagination!

There's no reason why a church (or group of churches) couldn't have a book club. Read one or two recommended books on a fairly regular basis and base the discussions round the issues raised. Invite others to be part of the group - not just church members.

Some groups are using resources like Steve Ayers' book, *What would Jesus say 2*[89] - and base discussions round the writers, presenters, celebrities and shows he looks at - Philip Pullman, Big Brother, Anne Robinson, Eminem, David Beckham, Robbie Williams all feature in this book.

We've already shown above how one church (J. John's) used clips from a film as the basis for a series of evening services. Some churches are now using clips as illustrations in their main morning diet of worship.Others are using material like that provided by *Connect Bible Studies* for small group meetings within their churches.

It might even be better if, as part of an outreach event or whatever, you can get a few church members to bring their friends and simply have a film night with a chance for snacks and chat at the end.

[89] Steve Ayers, *What would Jesus say* 2:, Inter-Varsity Press, 2003

Here's how the Bible Society describes its excellent web-based resource 'Reel Issues', encouraging people to chat about the big themes covered by many different movies:

> Stimulating group material to enable people at all stages of their spiritual journey to discuss how the Bible connects with the themes and stories in the latest talked-about films.

(See the Reel Issues homepage - find it through www.biblesociety.org.uk)

When Mel Gibson's *The Passion of the Christ* was released in March 2004, some churches made block bookings of entire cinemas so that church members could take their friends. There's no reason why a smaller group couldn't organise such an outing from time to time. Just about everyone seems to know about Dan Brown's best-selling novel *The Da Vinci Code*. I heard about one cathedral in England that organized a Da Vinci Nite - candles, music, drinks, a variety of contributions and time for discussion. Brilliant! Again, think of the opportunities when the film is released - sometime in 2006. Is the novel just a load of historically inaccurate hype? What is the Gospel of Thomas? Are the four gospels true? And wouldn't it be great if one of the cinema chains eventually allowed a local church to use their complex for Sunday worship? Comfy seats at last!

For Discussion

In what ways could you develop the ideas in this section?
– Book club?
Film club?
Use film clips in worship?

13. The Way of Jesus

Come, follow me and I will make you fishers of men.'
Jesus [90]

90 Mark 1:17

David

One possible paraphrase of Jesus' words is: 'You do the following. I'll do the making. Together we'll do the fishing.' This book has been about exploring that partnership with Jesus. If we follow him, he will transform us as we share in his mission.

Can we learn from Jesus about evangelism? Of course, we can. Is there a single obvious technique he used, or a pattern that can be detected? No, there isn't.

That's part of the secret - Jesus seems to treat each person differently. And that's the way it should be, because real people have different lives, different situations, different contexts, different problems, different needs, different personalities, different questions.

So we look now in a little more detail at a couple of encounters in the life of Jesus to see what clues they offer us about the ways we might share our faith with others.

The Woman at the Well (John 4:1 - 16)

This story is amazing for various reasons - Jews and Samaritans, for example, were supposed to hate each other; and apparently it wasn't kosher for a Jewish man to be speaking to a woman on her own anyway. So there's a 'starter for ten' - Jesus is never too bothered about breaking down barriers; he didn't allow the taboos of society to hold him back from sharing the good news of God's love.

And what does he do? Get his Bible out? No! He just asks her a question.
'Hi there! Any chance of a drink?'

Well, at least that how it starts! Once he's further into the conversation, he is prepared to throw out the occasional challenge and make the woman think. And apparently she gets round to sharing at a fair depth while he's taking a few mouthfuls of water…

Something special obviously happens, because she goes back to the town and manages to get a whole crowd out to meet Jesus, and 'many of the Samaritans from that town believed in him because of the woman's testimony … '(verse 39).

Once again, there's no one correct way of spreading the good news, but here are a few of the key ideas from this particular passage:

- Ask questions
- Listen
- Challenge people

Try it!

Here are some simple questions to drop into conversations you might be having with friends over coffee:

Did you ever say your prayers when you were a kid?

What do you think about life as you get older?

Have you ever been to church?

Any chance you could get the next round?

What did you think about that film?

Zacchaeus (Luke 19:1 - 10)

This story is useful because it helps dispel one of the great myths about Jesus and how he shared the good news. The myth is that Jesus was always preaching to large crowds of people and that's how he worked. And of course that's nonsense.

Yes, he preached to 'the multitudes', and as his reputation grew he was thronged by crowds; but there were other times when he went one-to-one with folk, 'homing in' on one person whose need seemed to be great - the woman who was bleeding to death for example (Mark 5).

'Who touched me?'

'Who touched you?' 'Oh, come on Jesus, the punters have come out in their hundreds today!'

'But some **ONE** touched me!'

Here's how Jesus works - he is interested in, and engages with **individuals.**

And to hammer this important point home, let's get back to 'the wee man' in Jericho. He's a wealthy wee man. Brilliant! Another myth dispelled - Jesus is only interested in poor people? No! Jesus loves the poor, the rich, the unwell, the healthy, children, adults. And we know Zacchaeus is a wee man because he has to climb a tree to get a good look at Jesus.

There must have been lots of decent, good-living folk there, but Jesus goes straight for the dirty cheatin' wee scum-bag of a tax collector, and says to him:
'A' right mate? You better come down. I'd like a cuppa at your place!'

(As you can see, I'm taking a bit of a liberty with the translation - this is the Glasgow version.)

But why does Jesus do that? Why does he spend a whole afternoon with **one individual**? And him a scum-bag! In his three-year ministry to change the world, he's only got a few hundred afternoons, and he spends the whole of one of them with this shady character.

That's the way Jesus works - with individuals.
He spends time with people. He listens to them. He asks questions. He challenges them. Can you do that? Yes, you can. Anyone can. It might take time. We've said earlier: this is a process. Don't rush. Relax. I like the way Michael Green puts it:

Evangelism is like rowing a boat round the island of someone's life until you find an appropriate place to land.[91]

Take it easy. Enjoy rowing. Angels can row. **'You're an Angel!'**

91 *Evangelism Today* audio-tape, York Courses, PO Box 343, York. YO 19 5YB

Peter, what story would you choose which shows Jesus as your role model in evangelism?

Peter

The Emmaus Road (Luke 24:13-35)

There's much to learn from Jesus about the art of post modern evangelism in the Emmaus road story. Here we meet people who are struggling with loss. Jesus walks and listens. He asks questions. He sets life in the story of the Messiah who suffers to enter his glory, and so gives meaning to the messy mystery of things. His words burn within them as authentic truth. He reveals his identity at a village supper table.

The Emmaus Road story offers clues on how to be church in a secular world. First, like the two disciples, we can be so obsessed by what we lack in our church life - status, members, young people - that, ironically, we are blind to the one vital resource we do have, who is alive and well and at our elbow.

Another clue offered by this story is in the significance of the places mentioned. The journey from Jerusalem to Emmaus may be seen as a journey away from the place of political power to the place of simplicity. European Christianity has had 1,700 years of alignment with power, and will find its renewal in a new simplicity.

The Emmaus Road is an invitation to be a simple church of 'strugglers anonymous', who drop the masks and take the way of the wounded healer. The simple church is not afraid to speak God's word that has first been lived out in our life together and then offered humbly to others with an authority born out of authenticity. The simple church will be a place of hospitality where the stranger finds a home and Christ arrives unexpectedly.

That story says it all.

Learning from Jesus
Jesus is the Way who meets people on the way.
Luke 24:13-35

Do you see yourself as able to meet others on the way inviting them to be followers of the Way?
Consider ways in which this could happen in your own day-to-day life.

Resources and acknowledgements

The publishers are grateful to the following for their permission to refer to or quote from the books listed. These books form an excellent resource base for further reading. We've also included some useful web addresses for more information.

Abraham, William,
The Logic of Evangelism, Hodder and Stoughton, 1991

Booker, Mike and Ireland, Mark,
Evangelism - which way now?, Church House Publishing, 2003

Finney, John,
*Emerging Evangelis*m, Darton Longman and Todd, 2004

Frost, Rob,
A Closer Look at New Age Spirituality, Kingsway, 2001

Fung, Raymond,
The Isaiah Agenda, WCC Publications, 1992

Hagberg, Janet O and Guelich, Robert A,
The Critical Journey - Stages in the Life of Faith, Word Publishing,1989

Hay, David & Hunt, Kay,
Understanding the Spirituality of People Who Don't Go to Church,
University of Nottingham, 2000

Holmes, John,
*Vulnerable Evangelism: The Way of Jesu*s, Grove Books Ltd - Ev 54, 2001

John. J and Stibbe, Mark,
The BIG PICTURE 2, Authentic Lifestyle, 2003

Manley Pippert, Rebecca,
*Out of the Saltshake*r, Inter-Varsity Press, 1980

McLaren, Brian D,
The Church on the Other Side - Doing Ministry in the Post-modern Matrix,
Zondervan, 2000

Newbigin, Lesslie,
*The Gospel in a Pluralist Societ*y, London: SPCK, 1989

Nouwen, Henri J M,
The Wounded Healer, Image Books, 1979

Nouwen, Henri J M,
Reaching Out - The Three Movements of the Spiritual Life, Fount, 1987

Nouwen, Henri JM,
Life of the Beloved: Spiritual Living in a Secular World,
Hodder and Stoughton,1993

Parsons, Rob,
Bringing Home the Prodigals, Hodder and Stoughton, 2003

Pinsky, Mark I,
The Gospel According to the Simpsons, Westminster John Knox Press, 2001

Reid, Gavin,
Redescribing Evangelism, British Council of Churches, 1989

Richmond, Yvonne, Nick Spencer, Anne Richards, Mark Ireland, Rob Frost
and Steven Croft
Evangelism in a Spiritual Age, Church House Publishing 2005

Tomlin, Graham,
The Provocative Church, SPCK, 2002

Sjogren, Steve,
Conspiracy of Kindness, Vine Books, 1993

Spencer, Nick,
Beyond Belief? Barriers and Bridges to Faith Today,
The London Institute for Contemporary Christianity, 2003

Warren,Rick,
The Purpose Driven Church, Grand Rapids, MI: Zondervan, 1995

Websites
www.businessalphaedinburgh.com
www.oasisedinburgh.com
www.rejesus.com
www.businessinglasgow.net
www.worktalk.co.uk
www.rejesus.co.uk

The Authors

A Word about David

David was born in Glasgow and brought up in East Kilbride. Before going into the parish ministry, he worked for Rolls Royce aero-engine manufacturers, initially in the metallurgy lab, then as a production engineer and finally as a development engineer.

In his home church (Moncreiff Parish Church) he was president of the youth fellowship, a member of the summer mission team (to North Berwick, then Stranraer) and an elder. He accepted the call to the parish ministry and served East Kilbride West Kirk as minister from 1983 to 2000, when he took up the post of Senior Adviser in Mission and Evangelism for the Church of Scotland. He is married to Gwen and they have two sons and two daughters - David, Jennifer, Merle and John.

He finds golf a most frustrating game, but enjoys hill-walking, skiing, swimming, music, having a drink with friends and travelling around on his motor bike.

A Word from David

It was a tremendous privilege to be asked to write a book such as this. For me, it has been decidedly therapeutic; it has given me the opportunity to share many of the stories which have meant so much to me over the years; and not least, it has given me the opportunity of collaborating with a much respected colleague. Well, I can say that now, but when the project was first mentioned, Peter and I wondered how we were going to fit our 'pet material' together! But there's another wee 'miracle' for you. It's all out there now for the Lord to use as he will and you'll hardly be able to tell what's his and what's mine! (His is the bit that's wrote proper!)

As always, Peter constantly offered his own blend of encouragement. But the whole thing started when a friend, Ian Gilmour, suggested this contribution as the right kind of book for our church at this time. The traditional churches are still in steep decline numerically, and the Church of Scotland is no different, but there are still thousands of Christians all over our country and miracles are happening when folk discover their full potential for sharing God's love. In the course of my work with local congregations all over Scotland, I've met plenty of 'angels'.

I would never have got round to doing this unless certain people had spurred me on - good friends like Billy and Gwen who allow my wife and me to retreat to their Argyll home on a regular basis (it helps us keep our sanity). And the team of advisers in Mission and Evangelism who prayed for us and made work so much fun. I've already mentioned Ian and Peter and there are so many others, I'll not be able to mention them all.

Thank you to the congregation (East Kilbride West Kirk) where I was minister and where I needed 'angels' to be patient with my mistakes. Thank you to the Board of National Mission for giving me study leave to be able to commit to this work; thank you to friends who allowed me to use their stories.

Thank you to other colleagues in the Church of England who have been a support and inspiration - Robert Warren allowed me to use some of his ideas; John Young sent me any amount of material from the *York Courses*; Robin Gamble allowed me to use *Leading Your Church into Growth* (his pub outreach in Bradford and *Gospel according to the Beatles* were an inspiration).

And thanks to the 'angels' who put up with me day in and day out - my wife and family.

David E. P. Currie

A Word about Peter

Peter Neilson also hails from Lanarkshire, where he was nurtured in his faith at Kirkmuirhill Church through all the usual patterns of church life. He owes more than he can say to a host of 'angels' who made that church a great place to be - and above all a place to meet the living Christ.

After education in Hamilton and Glasgow, he studied theology in Edinburgh, and was trained at Dunblane Cathedral for two and a half years before entering his first charge in Mount Florida, Glasgow. When that great congregation had taught him as much as he was willing to learn, he then led the first team of Advisers in Mission and Evangelism and combined that with being Director of Training at St Ninian's, Crieff. These were privileged years of meeting God's 'angels' all over Scotland and beyond.

Convinced of the need to listen to people outside the church, and look at new patterns of communication and Christian community for a new generation, he became Associate Minister at St Cuthbert's in Edinburgh city centre, responsible for mission strategy in the worlds of business, clubbing and homelessness.

Currently, he works with the Board of National Mission, supporting initiatives in church planting under the Committee on New Charge Development.

Peter has been married to Dorothy for 34 years, and is father to Pauline, Jane and Susan. Pauline is married to a Church of Scotland minister and Jane is married to an Episcopal priest, so they are an ecumenical family. He is a proud grandfather to Skye.

He prays that this book will ensure that Skye's generation will hear clearly the story of Jesus and become a host of 'angels' who pass it on in their own way.

A Word from Peter

This has been a new venture for me - to write a book at all!
It has been made much easier by having David as a partner
in crime. My ministry has been based on the premise that it
takes a community of God's people to communicate the good
news about the God of love. That means that ministry is always
about teamwork based on mutual respect and trust - and
accountability.

These qualities have been at the heart of this enterprise as we
have moved from the first nervous 'splurge' of ideas to watching
the Genesis One miracle recur before our eyes, as the Spirit
brought order out of mutually generated chaos!

We had to trust each other with unfinished thoughts and watch
while we each shaped and reshaped the material into the
finished article. Neither of us would have stayed the course
without the smiling encouragement of our editor, Janet de Vigne
at Scottish Christian Press. She never doubted us. It was a
challenge to live up to her faith in us! Thank you, Janet. You are
an angel!

Most of my new ventures in ministry have been because
somebody kicked me in the right place and in the right direction.
Thanks to Ian Gilmour for being the man with the golden boot!
If there is anything worthwhile in this book, it is thanks to the
many people who have generously poured their wisdom, faith,
compassion and insights into me over the years. I can see
many faces and hear many voices who are part of that great
company of God's people who have loved me, nurtured me,
confronted me, corrected me, infuriated me, frustrated me and
by God's grace have nudged me further along the way with
Jesus.

Thanks to you all - not least to those who do sing now with the
real angels before the throne of God and our Lord Jesus Christ!

Peter Neilson

Printed in the United Kingdom
by Lightning Source UK Ltd.
126283UK00002B/73-99/A

9 781905 022267